A Healthy Thing Should Look Like This!

A Minister's musings.....

.....in Shorts!

R F Pennington

Copyright 2012 by the author of this book, R F Pennington.
The book author retains sole copyright
to his contributions to this book.

Published 2010.
Second Edition. Published 2012.
Printed in the United States of America by Lightning Source Inc.

All Scripture quotations are from the New American Standard Bible
© 1975, Lockman Foundation. All Greek Dictionary citings © 1981,
Lockman Foundation. Reproduction permission granted through
Foundation Press Publications, publisher for the
Lockman Foundation.

This book published by BookCrafters,
Joe and Jan McDaniel.
SAN 859-6352
bookcrafters@comcast.net

ISBN 978-1-937862-29-9
Library of Congress Control Number 2012920248

Copies of this book may be ordered at
www.bookcrafters.net
and other online bookstores.

Dedication

To David Kohn, my brother in Christ and spiritual giant. The one who encouraged me to take the great leap into the ministry decades ago. Both of us have experienced bumpy rides. We get separated by time and distance (he and Liz are currently lost somewhere in the Deep South), but those times we do get together to laugh and think, I feel refreshed and recharged. I can only imagine it is the same feeling people got long years ago who were privileged enough to sit under a shade tree and simply visit with Jesus.

David makes me laugh. He also makes me think--and think deep. Love you, Brother. I hope this makes you laugh. You've been there, much more than I have. Keep your eyes on The Lord, and a straight path towards the coal pile!

And the LORD opened the mouth of the donkey, and she said to Balaam, "What have I done to you, that you have struck me these three times?" Then Balaam said to the donkey, "Because you have made a mockery of me! If there had been a sword in my hand, I would have killed you by now." Numbers 22

Table of Contents

Foreword 1

Funerals 4

MSG Freezes 11

All the Cats of the Bible 20

Minister's Feet 29

Hitchhikers 33

She Liked Fudge! 39

TechnoWorship 44

Airports in the Circle of Life 53

Bus Twilight Zone 64

The Gate Keepers 75

Micaiah 91

King of Burns 100

Concluding Question 114

Foreword

No, I have not lost my mind. Not completely yet. Some of you may be wondering just what a Healthy Thing is. Others of you are trying to fake it by telling other people, "Oh, sure, I see these Healthy Things all the time. Usually come out after a rain. Sometimes they run out on the road after dark and you have to flash your lights..."

Seems that back in High School, my oldest son was sitting next to a girl who pulled out one of those little pencil bags that students use to house pencils, erasers, a small stapler and other assorted odds and ends that High Schoolers feel compelled to carry around. It was fuzzy and looked like its father might have been a piece of shag carpet from the late sixties, early seventies. My son told her it looked like a sick animal. He then drew this Healthy Thing and noted under it that a Healthy Thing Should Look Like This! If you look closely, you can see the zipper on its side.

And I have held on to this picture for almost a decade. Because one of my kids drew it? Well, primarily the answer is no. I've hung onto the picture because it makes me laugh. We need to laugh. It is like the picture that my youngest son drew while sitting in a pew one Sunday morning. I was preaching a sermon out of John chapter six. My wife was listening and my youngest was very intently drawing. When Dee looked, it was a picture of a slice of bread with arms and legs--dancing. When Mom asked what the picture was all about, our youngest replied, "This is the Bread of Life, just like Daddy is preaching about!"

What about the birdlike creature next to the Bread of Life? It's the Seraphim out of Isaiah chapter six. Connected? Yep, read John 12:41 and connect the dots. Evidently a kid in kindergarten did. He was listening to the Preacher and taking notes...they just happened to be illustrative!

So, this is a collection of Ministerial Shorts. Now, I didn't call them Ministerial Short Stories. The subtitle is on purpose. My particular brand of church growing up didn't allow the wearing of shorts, so even the title makes me laugh. Couldn't play cards, either. And hanging out at the swimming pool could really take away points needed to make it into Heaven!

As disciples, we tend to gravitate toward the point system for some reason.

We need to laugh. As the redeemed, we should be THE MOST HAPPY of folks that are running around Planet Here. Sometimes we act as if it's a sin to grin or like we've been baptized in vinegar and weaned on sauerkraut. We need to show emotion. There are just some things in life that ought to move even the most hardened brother or sister, when injustice is done to one human from another--especially when done for the sake of a twisted laugh or out of indifference. We need to be reminded that we are humans and we're surrounded by other humans on this spinning ball of carbon. Sometimes these facts alone can bring us to the verge of tears. I was moved in that direction in a few of these stories myself. You may be, also.

Therefore, if you were ever wondering just what goes through the mind of a Minister (or at least through this one's mind), well, here you have it. And above all, these stories are to help remind us that we always need to put our Bible knowledge to good use as we go through our Monday morning to Saturday night routines--or those special times like a funeral or waiting in a bus station for our trip home. Sitting in a pew on Sunday morning, feeling jacked up like a spiritual Samson is only a tiny fraction of the week. Come Monday morning we hit the world and we go about our rat killing and by the time Saturday afternoon rolls around we can almost hear the clouds roll back and a voice proclaiming (alongside a giant finger pointing out of the clouds right towards us), "O ye of little faith!"

Finally, some of these stories are just plain dumb. Not stupid dumb, but a, "My mind is pretty numb right now and

I need a little brainless something to read right about now." Well, if brainless is the order of the evening, then you can't go wrong with this book. I had to take a break from lessons.

Keep in mind the Two Sided Jack Corollary: All work and no play makes Jack a dull boy. All play and no work makes Jack broke!

What?!

Enjoy!

Funerals

"Blessed are the dead who die in the Lord from now on!"
"Yes," says the Spirit, "so that they may rest from their labors, for their deeds follow with them." John's Revelation

There is, perhaps, no sadder time than that which we call a funeral. We lose pets as children, but that doesn't even begin to prepare us for life's greatest heart ache. It is a grieving time, when we say, "Good-bye" to someone that was close to us in life. It is not a "See you later this afternoon," or even a "I'll see you next spring," but a permanent farewell (Or not permanent. Depends on where you are headed and where they just landed.) to that person and the totality of their life here on earth. As a minister, I witnessed and participated in dozens of these final acts. Some were 'expected.' Some were not. All were tragic, and left families undone for months to come. All deaths leave holes.

Often times the last picture that we have of that person, friend or relative is the eternal picture of their body laid out in state, as folks file by to pay their last respects and farewells. Flowers garnish the final resting place of the body that will, in time, return to the dust of the ages just as the flowers lining the casket turn brown and are finally discarded. Our minds close in on that final afternoon as words that we cannot even hear are being said on behalf of the dearly departed--and on behalf of the survivors, those who must somehow continue to live their life day after day, accepting and dealing with the void that is indelibly left in our lap.

It can also be a rip-roarious time, if you knew Granny.

No, not *my* Granny. She was everyone's Granny. Actually,

A Minister's Musing...in Shorts!

she was old enough to be quite a number of people's great-Granny. My, what a full life. Outlived a number of husbands, starting with a soldier boy, wed almost to the moment the young man stepped on the train ultimately bound for the trenches of the First World War. Like nearly an entire generation, he never returned. There were others, whom she outlived also. Finally, in the last light of her lifetime, I had the privilege of meeting Granny. She was bedfast and dying of cancer, but had a sound faith and an alert mind. Granny knew what was in store for her across the Jordan--but no one would let her make plans for this eternal vacation!

Part of the job description of the local preacher is to assist those who are about to make that one way journey. Granny was no exception. Often I would go and sit by her bedside for an afternoon here and there. As the conversation evolved, it always shifted toward the ultimate journey. It would always shift right back again as soon as the omnipresent care givers, known as the Ensure People, would enter the room. A verbal tug of war would ensue.

"What?! Oh, my! Granny, what on earth are you two talking about in here?"

"I'm not talking about anything on earth. I'm talking with my Pastor about going to Heaven if you don't mind too terribly."

"Oh, Granny, we're all going to go to Heaven some day. I just don't think that we need to talk about it. Here, drink your Ensure. It will make you strong."

"Now, if you were going to go to North Carolina, you would make arrangements, wouldn't you? You would make some sort of verbal plans, wouldn't you?"

"Oh, now Granny you know that the doctors won't let you go to North Carolina. You need to rest and get your strength. Here, drink your Ensure. It will make you strong."

"I don't want any Ensure, at least not that Vanilla stuff. Makes me ill and gives me gas. Tastes bad. Besides, I'm not going to get any better. I'm dying, in case you didn't hear the doctors last time they were in here. Dying. D-Y-I-N-G spells dying and there isn't a dang thing you or anyone else can do about it. Let me talk to my preacher about some things."

"Oh," --and here is where I would get that look. That

same look your mother used to give you when you were eight years old and cutting up in public or kicking the table legs at a dinner party-- "Brother Pennington was just leaving. Have a nice day, Brother Pennington. Call before you come back." ...and I would find myself standing on the front porch, door closing, wondering just what had happened to me.

And so it went. I'm not sure that we ever got around to talking about Heaven in detail. I'm also dead sure that we never fully got around to discussing songs and favorite Bible passages that Granny wanted to have read and sung at her funeral. We did, one day, get a good laugh about who had the cheapest funeral planned. Granny was just sure that no one could ever get a cheaper burial than she had already arranged, and went into great detail to explain. No lead lined caskets in concrete vaults with a satin lining. No fancy headstone with little naked cherubs chiseled on the top. No brass lettering inset on the stone. No fancy crushed velvet casket liner. Bottom line stuff--rock bottom. She then would wave a feeble hand in an 'Igotcha' manner and dare me to outdo that one.

I told her that just before I died I was to tell my wife, then get into a giant lawn and leaf bag and hop out to the dumpster. She would push me in the rest of the way and close the lid. Granny couldn't top that one 'cause Granny couldn't hop. But we did get the biggest, side splitting laugh you ever heard or will hope to. We really got to rolling, when the Ensure Lady once again tossed me out with a look and a 'Brother-Pennington-was-just-leaving.' Once again, like a cat being tossed out before bedtime, I had no idea just how I got onto the front porch.

In short, one did not go to Granny's house to 'visit' her, like someone on your shopping list to cross off. One did not go to Granny's house to comfort her or be there for her or any of the other euphemisms we use. You went to Granny's house for good ol' fashioned conversation and fun. You *were* going to come away from her house feeling like you've had a laugh.

By and by, I got the call. One sort of knows in the ministry that when the phone rings at 11:37 at night that it won't be good. Same as being the parent of teenagers. A sadness. A sense of relief. A sense of loss. A two month's supply of Ensure. It was time for Granny to go elsewhere to do other things for the rest of eternity. The family was alerted. Suitcases were packed and thrown into cars. Pizza was ordered. Tuesday morning finally arrived as I stepped through the church house doors. It was Granny's going away day.

Funeral home folks are a different breed of cat.

Somewhere they go to school, I'm sure, to get their poker faces and empathetic voices. Soft organ music seems to follow them around, much like the music in the produce section at the grocery store. No one is sure where it comes from. Ceiling? A peach? As the preacher, it was my duty to unlock the church building early so that they could come in and set Granny and her flowers up for all to say farewell--and then eat lunch.

To work in a funeral home, one must learn to walk with the hands folded together, one over the other, just about crotch level, coat buttoned and not a hair out of place. Arms just *do not swing* when you walk and work for a funeral home. While sitting in my office (playing Mine Sweeper on the computer, I'm sure), I was faintly aware of two funeral home types approaching my office door.

"Reverend, we have the decedent's casket available for your viewing if you would like to spend a few moments in silence before anyone else arrives." These guys were, pardon the pun, deathly serious. It was time to walk.

Being the Reverend of the day, I slowly arose from my chair and made my way out of my office and toward the ultimate viewing. I felt like a prisoner walking the last mile as I made my way down the hall into the main chapel, accompanied by one man in black on the right and one man in black on the left. I swung my arms as I walked. I approached the open casket.

"OH Gr-Gr-Granny!" I began to sob loudly as I dropped to my knees, clutching the side of the casket with one hand and grasping the non-satin liner tightly with the other. Without so much as a facial wrinkle moving on their starched faces, each man produced a small travel-type package of facial tissues as each one offered me a chance to partake of theirs. I turned it off, stood up and said, "Just kidding guys! Man, she's as dead as Julius Caesar!"

They broke.

They broke with the kind of spontaneous laugh that causes a man to lift his foot, stomp the ground and slap his thigh at the same time. I knew they had it in them and it wasn't a 24 hour a day thing, otherwise you would be able to pick these guys out in J.C. Penny's or Burger King all the time. Both laughed till tears started rolling down their faces. This is the way Granny would have wanted it, but the best is yet to come: the Ensure People were about to make their debut to check that everything was right and to the ready. It was the last time that day that the funeral home folks would find *anything* funny.

Now, I'm just willing to bet that Funeral Home People go to a lot of trouble setting things up for a funeral. There are caskets to carry in and open. There are liners and ruffles to smooth out. There are dozens of flower stands and flower pots and statues and cards and mementos and guest books and memorial brochures to arrange--whatever you call those things. You men always slip them into your coat pocket, the coat you always wear only to funerals. Next funeral, while fidgeting around in the pew like you're in a straightjacket, you fish it out and say, "Man, have they been dead that long? Seems like only yesterday!" Hopefully, you say it to yourself so your wife doesn't poke you.

While setting up for a funeral service, the speaker must be taken into consideration. The logistics of entry and exit and parking and procession must be kept in mind. Flower petals must be picked up as flowers are paraded to and fro. In short, a one or two hour nightmare must be surmounted. They had done their best in Granny's case, but they were soon to find out that their best just wasn't good enough for the Ensure People as they made their entry into the chapel.

"Now who on earth decided that this would all be this way? Was it you? I thought we talked about it!" The two Ensure People gave each other the 'look.' It was the look that, I'm just sure, the coxswain gave the captain of the Titanic just before they contacted that giant ice cube.

"Lands, I thought that we would have her out in the foyer for viewing, then put her down here. I think we discussed this all yesterday. Uh-huh, I think we did. Yep, we did."

Another look swapped between Ensure People, this time with a different flavor.

"Oh, sirs! We've decided that we would like to have her in the foyer for viewing as people come in so that they can pay their last respects 'cause some folks don't like to go filing down front after the service 'cause they get kinda uncomfortable sometimes and Uncle Cletus can't walk good and neither can ol' Emma 'cause she's got gout never mind that she's overweight and would it be too much trouble to move all of this if you know what I mean thank you very much?"

"No, ma'am. No trouble at all."

Saying "No trouble at all" was a kind way of saying that the Ensure People had asked that the Funeral Home People remove an hour's work and put it all back together in a blink of an eye. In short, magic! However, with the patience of Job they began the slow, meticulous task of removing flowers from the casket, refolding the ruffled non-satin liner, closing the lid and slowly marching Granny through the long main chapel.

One pushed the casket and the other walked slowly behind with his hands straight down at his side. Flowers and cards and statues and mementos would comprise the next several trips. Reparked and repatriated with her flowers, Granny was now available once again for review in the church house foyer.

"Oh, my! I wonder if it was Mabel who wanted Granny down in the front of the main chapel? Did anyone talk to Mabel? Oh, my! I feel like this whole thing is out of control! Mabel would be hurt if we didn't talk to her."

"Well, I don't think that Mabel would care one way or the other. This is just what we decided on and that's that. It's done now. We just have to make decisions at a time like this and we made a decision and no one else is here to make a decis…"

"Maybe *Harold* talked to them!" And with that, a moment of decided silence between the two of them, simultaneously shocked at the chance that *Harold* may have something to do with the previous placement of Granny and her paraphernalia.

"Lands o' Goshen! I'll bet Harold did talk to them! I wonder if Harold told them to put Granny the way she was? You're right. I'll just bet that it was Harold. Harold would know what was best. Harold is good in these situations."

Then a pause while the Ensure People look intently at one another, as a sign of solidarity after the big breakthrough thought of the day. Through some sort of feminine telepathy, a spokesman was chosen.

"Oh, sirs, would you mind putting her back in the chapel?"

Whatever you think about funeral home people, one has to feel sorry for them at this time: refolding the liner, closing the lid, removing the flowers from the casket top and slowly starting the Granny parade all over again. But, alas, this move was not to be Granny's last. However, this was to be the next to the last move wherein the funeral home people took the extra care in folding the liner, closing the lid and removing the flowers. From then on it was hood up and go baby, go!

The last several moves looked more like a soap box derby. Rattled funeral home people pushing an open casket up and down the aisles and hallways of the church building with such speed and precision that not only were their ties blowing behind them, but they were maneuvering corners with great precision. I even witnessed hands swinging slightly as they walked, no, ran from point to point. At points along the straight away, it seemed that mach one was approached as flower petals exploded off the stems. Being wholly intrigued by all of this, I couldn't help myself when I stepped in during momentary pauses in the derby to say something to the Ensure People like "What about Mabel?" or "You *did* talk to Harold, didn't you?" Had the funeral home folks over heard me, I'm sure they would have ambushed me later in the day and beaten me with a sand sock.

I did notice that each time Granny came in for another lap that she had the same smile on her face that I had grown to love and enjoy over the last year.

MSG Freezes

So then, some were shouting one thing and some another, for the assembly was in confusion and the majority did not know for what reason they had come together. **Acts 19:32**

I got real busy when I was in full time ministry. At times I didn't know if I was coming or going. I'm pretty sure I met myself on several occasions throughout my tenure. I had funerals, weddings, baby blessings, sermons, classes, letters to write, phone calls to make, hospital visits to make in several cities and multiple hospitals, and eat in there somewhere. A church secretary was a must, a Godsend!

One Tuesday, I spent quite a bit of time trying to cipher a sticky note stuck to my computer screen by my secretary. It read, *MSG's from machine* and was attached to many other sticky notes plastered right in the middle of my monitor.

Sticky notes are curious things. I could get up from my desk and pursue a drink of water, a cup of coffee or a stretch break and there would be a fresh batch of stickies lining my monitor. Never mind the fact that our computers were etherneted together and she could have texted me a note that would have popped up immediately on my screen. No, the stickies still lived. They might be yellow, pink, turtle shaped, small, medium or large. This little trip to refill Joe yielded no exception, but usually I could figure out what was going on. This time I couldn't, and it made me uncomfortable. Large things were at stake.

Was this note intentionally cryptic, to once again prove to me that I wasn't the one running the show around the office? Let's be real here. Anyone with a secretary who they lean on with any regularity knows that it is much less a hassle (and long term damage done) to make your wife mad. Secretaries were, are, and will be indispensable for centuries to come. I needed to understand MSG. Grasp that, and the machine part would fall into my lap--or so I thought.

After much thoughtfulness, I was pretty sure it wasn't the food preservative monosodium glutamate. Had I been a restaurant owner, food buyer or nutritionist in a large hospital, that would be a viable option. However, I was the minister for a fairly good sized congregation in the Pacific Northwest. Since the church deals with people and not chemicals, I scratched my tiny brain for anyone who had those initials. A quick search of the church database resulted in only one person in the G's--and it wasn't anywhere close to MSG. I then turned my attention to any machines we might have around the building--copy machine, coffee machine, bread machine, eMachine, and I soon exhausted the list. After all, we were well into the middle of the 20th century (even though my calendar said 2001) and had, sort of, the latest and greatest stuff. Nothing that would fit MSG.

I thought about the translation of the Bible called The Message. After all, I reminded myself, this IS a church that concentrates on spiritual matters and Bible things. Never mind that the sticky was stuck to the days **MeSsaGes** from the *answering* machine--I couldn't figure it out! I had to get up, go into the office next door and humble myself before my secretary. It was then I realized that, for whatever reason, I had fallen for one of the oldest things around. I was Oblivious to the Obvious.

Human beings fall for stuff all the time. Even way back when, mankind was falling for things--and did. Imagine living in a garden with everything going well and all of a sudden, out of the blue, this snake whom you heretofore had not known wants to talk to you and be your friend...

Oblivious to the Obvious is also a disease among humans from time to time. It can (if we are the observer and not the oblivious one) cause us to squeal with delight for hours and days. It can also (if we are the oblivious one and others are the observers) cause us to want to spend the majority of the work day in the company bathroom or under our desk or some other private place. Too bad, and we want to go live in a cave and hunt deer the rest of our natural existence.

A Minister's Musing...in Shorts!

Sometimes *everyone* in a group, no matter the size, is oblivious to the obvious. I remember one such event while 4-Wheeling the deserts of Southeast New Mexico with my wife. As any reader who has children will know and immediately recognize, this is stuff that takes place B.C.--Before Children. After Diapers, or A.D., simply will not allow happenings like this for many years to come. To make sense of the senselessness, I will need to describe a bit of the surroundings and some background information.

During that time, we both worked for the same major oil company. She as a geologist and I as a drilling supervisor. Both of us prided ourselves on knowing the oil field in our respective disciplines. In case you are wondering just what I'm trying to say, I'll put it in plain language--we were hot stuff. One thing we both knew how to do was to read abandoned well markers.

By law, any abandoned oil or gas well needed to be plugged from the bottom up, and the finality of the abandonment was a four inch diameter steel pipe with the lease name and location of the well welded onto the pipe for all eternity--or at least a very long time. We knew the 'oil patch' like our own backyard. Give me a township and range, and I could tell you where I was, how far to the next town and what that next town was! She could do the same. We also had almost every lease name memorized by heart. Most were named for people. There was the E. E. Wilson, the W. W. Mullins, the W. A. Slaughter, the State TZ, and the one which won the distinction of being the longest to have to write into log books every day was the White City Penn Gas Federal Com Unit, which happened to be just outside the mouth of Carlsbad Caverns National Park-- you know, the bat cave, but that's another story.

Well, there we were 4-wheeling our way around Antelope Ridge in our new Ford Bronco having the time of our life. A turn here and a dip there and pretty soon we became, should we say, disoriented. Not lost, mind you, but just severely disoriented. A series of hills and vales and no trees to look at, it can become a place where you can say, "That's west, all right," but it does you no good. It is then when we looked in the distance and saw an oxidized four inch diameter steel pole sticking five feet out of the ground. We were soon going to be on our way home as we four wheeled into the distance to meet the steel 'road map' back home.

I got out and began to make out the rusty letters and numbers. With most leases reflecting the names of the landowners that were originally alive when the first well was drilled, I was expecting two initials followed by a last name.

"What does it say?"

"I'm making it out. Hang onto your britches a minute. Let me brush some rust and junk off of it (Remember, there are no trees on Antelope Ridge. Nothing for the birds to sit on except these abandoned well markers). First letter is F. Yep, it's an F all right!"

"Off hand, I can't think of a lease that begins with an F anywhere around here, can you?."

"No, I can't either but the next letter is an E. Then a D-E-R… hang on…A-I , no,L."

"It's the F. E. Deral? I don't know of any F. E. Deral leases."

"Yep. Let me look again. F-E …D-E-R-A-L. I don't guess I've ever heard of that one, either?

"No. Gee whiz, I've looked extensively at maps in this area. That one must be a waaaay old one, drilled way back when they first started finding oil around here back before the Great Depression. What's the date on it?"

"Looks like 1979. Hmm, not so old after all. I think Texaco drilled around here, but I've never heard of it either."

Please, dear reader, get the mental image of two young people in the prime of their life, degrees running out their ears and over 400 semester hours of college between the two of them. Silhouetted against the New Mexico sky, no less.

Of course by the time that we finally put it together and figured out that it was a Federal lease, we felt like doofs. Oblivious to the obvious. However, now we are faced with another factor known as the Multiple Doofing.

You well know how those multiple doofings go. You've had to deal with them more often that you would like to admit or remember. Pretty soon one doof is pitted against the other, knowing that both doofs have acted ignorantly, but needing to exonerate so as to make the other doof look more ignorant in the long run. Lickety-split, and we were off on each other so as to create Major Doof and Minor Doof:

"I could have figured it out if you would have read the letters faster to me!"

"I wasn't reading, I was scratching and cyphering letters through rust!"

These are the humorous doofings all the while being oblivious to the obvious. There comes a time when that oblivion can become dangerous.

Several years ago we went on one of those mega vacations that we swore a thousand times that we would never take again. You know the type that takes you all over the universe, and you end up doing things that you wouldn't normally do, spending money you don't have. While on this vacation, we spent some time, and money, in a petting zoo in the Texas hill country. Now my children that were left at home were long past the age of the petting zoo, but this was one of those type of vacations when you find yourself just doing it for no particular reason.

Entry into the main area with my nearly-taller-than-Mama sons slinking around trying not to be seen by anyone they might know (you never know who will pop up a couple of thousand miles from home at a petting zoo!). A young girl of about six, with long dark hair, was busy running first from this goat and then to that pig, trying to poke little pre-formed green food pellets down their throats. She was also being followed around by a llama who was trying his best to have her hair as the main course. She was so intent on feeding the goats and pigs and rabbits and whatever those other things were, that she was Oblivious to the Obvious. Each time she slowed down to toss pellets at pigs, the llama would suck up somewhere between a small bit or a great bunch of her hair, like spaghetti through a straw, and begin to roll it around in his little llama mouth, which had recently been used for other things.

First, one of our boys tried to tell her to watch out, that a llama was trying to eat her hair. She didn't give him much more than a glance. I personally rescued her hair out of the llama's mouth on two subsequent occasions. Each time we were careful not to overstep our bounds and play parent. However, out of the dozens of folks in and around the pen, we couldn't tell exactly who was whose and which belonged to whom. She looked, for all practical purposes, like an abandoned child, though a petting zoo in the Texas hill country would be a strange place for that to have been carried out. Each time that we tried our best to kindly intervene, she looked at us as if we had come from Mars and were trying to deal her some kind of misery. As it turned out, English wasn't her bag so all she saw were a few strangers pushing on her, grabbing her hair and saying unintelligible things. Meanwhile, her hair looked more and more like it had been wiped down with some sort of oat bran mush.

Sometimes we don't quite recognize when bad is coming, or where it is coming from. Sometimes those who are trying to help are seen as doing the harm or the bad. Oftentimes, confusion of the moment brings about snap decisions in our mind and other understandings simply because we want to remove the question mark of what is actually going on at the time--and we find ourselves oblivious to the obvious.

Sometimes the outcome is minor and humorous. Sometimes it is major, crumpling lifelong friendships and damaging lives.

All in all, we are stuck on this planet and are surrounded by one another, which means that we must somehow deal with one another. There are several ways to do just that. We can deal harshly, by making ourselves the center of our universe and in the demanding that the other planets revolve around our agenda, create fallout and shooting stars. Or, we can choose another way. This is where the Proverbs come in.

Now, I don't know what you think about the Book of Proverbs, or even the Bible as a whole. Some hold it as the Book of all books, some hold it as little more than a farce. I choose the former. Still others see it as a mysterious collection that may or may not be from the mouth and mind of God Himself (still some are wondering how llamas and rusty well markers can create a jump to a moral). Either way, one cannot argue with the Proverbs.

I can pull some Theological Magic from my long ago seminary days and say that the content of the Book of Proverbs is in fact a Hebraic collection of antithetical parallelisms, or I can keep it down to earth and say that they are short sayings with a punch. The punch comes when one reads not very far into the Proverbs and suddenly sees that these sayings were written with the reader in mind. Which reader?

Any reader who dares to read them.

Probably anyone who has ventured into the Proverbs has started out first thinking of this person and then that. It is only when your circle of people is exhausted, that you will realize that the book is about YOU. For ten years in a row I made it a habit to read the Proverbs once a year in one sitting. I did this each year on my annual sabbatical trip to the Holy Land while scrunched up in an airliner seat. Some think that the Holy Land is somewhere in the Middle East around Palestine. I assure you it is in Lubbock, Texas.

Start reading it and you will soon see that the book is not to be outlined. It isn't as simple as "Chapter one is about...and chapter two deals with . . ." It is simply one punchy saying after another, but begins and ends with wisdom. Well, why not? Isn't that what we ultimately want to be known for? The things we know and how to use those things?

We're not all going to make a million. We're not all going to run the company. We're not all going to own the lion's share of the stock. But we do want to be known for our brains. Our wisdom. Not facts. Not a walking encyclopedia, but the WISE use of knowledge, which is what wisdom is. Heaven forbid that we go through life saying dumb things like, "F. E. Deral," and have llamas eating our hair.

The book almost begins with the statement, "The fear of the Lord is the beginning of knowledge. Fools despise wisdom and instruction." Well, take it or leave it on the first sentence-- God will straighten that out with you later if you miss that one. But has anything been more true than the second sentence? I've taught some old dogs at least not to chew up the carpet, but you can't tell the village idiot anything. Why? Because they have some sort of narcissistic hatred of having ANYONE tell them ANYTHING about ANYTHING. Why? Because the universe revolves around them, just ask them. Now talk about oblivious to the obvious!

We're going to go through life scratching rust off of abandoned well markers, then shifting blame when we find

A Healthy Thing Should Look Like This!

out we've done something dumber than mud. We will go around life, at times, with plastered, slimy hair, smiling at everyone who is frantically trying to chase the llamas away. There are just going to be those times when we are standing there saying, "What?!" and the world around us will be retorting, "Duh!" But let me leave you with these particular quotes out of the Proverbs for your kicking around. If it sparks your interest, read the entire thing on your next flight to the Holy Land--or the next time you are scouring the house for something to read.

The way of a fool is right in his own eyes, but a wise man is he who listens to counsel.

Wisdom is in the presence of the one who has understanding, but the eyes of a fool are on the ends of the earth.

I passed by the field of the sluggard, and by the vineyard of the man lacking sense. It was completely overgrown with thistles, its surface was covered with nettles, and its stone wall was broken down. When I saw, I reflected upon it. I looked, and received instruction. "A little sleep, a little slumber, a little folding of the hands to rest, then your poverty will come as a robber, and your want like an armed man."

Every prudent man acts with knowledge, but a fool displays folly.

Keeping away from strife is an honor for a man, but any fool will quarrel.

Do not answer a fool according to his folly, lest you also be like him. (By the way, your mother always told you this one, except she said, "Don't get down on their level.")

The sluggard is wiser in his own eyes than seven men who can give a discreet answer.

A fool always loses his temper, but a wise man holds it back.

A fool does not delight in understanding, but only in revealing his own mind.

The sluggard says, "There is a lion outside! I shall be slain in the streets!"

That last one is my all-time favorite. If you are lazy, I guess one excuse is as good as another when you're trying to get out of work. Lions outside. Really! Try the Proverbs. Proverbs is good stuff.

All the Cats of the Bible

This section really doesn't have anything to do with the Bible except that cats are mentioned in the Bible somewhere. I can't remember if it is in the Old Testament or the New Testament. Didn't someone own a thousand cats in Babylon or Damascus in First or Second Chronicles? Or was it one of the Apostles had a cat, or maybe Peter's mother-in-law in Mark chapter one? Maybe cats were on the list in Revelation 22:15 of those who were outside? No, that was dogs only, at least as far as any animals listed. Anyway, cats are a biblical subject so we will explore them here.

Actually, I've just been told that cats are *not* mentioned in the Bible at all. See, it IS good to have a great church secretary! However, it is a great story that you will want to tell around a campfire or to your grandchildren, so let's get on with it.

I've wondered about something since I was a kid. Now, mind you I have this sort of pretty good memory. Not what you would call a true photographic memory, just a pretty darn good one. For instance, I can remember everyone in my kindergarten class. OK, so they were also my first grade, second grade, third grade and so on, but a pretty good memory, nonetheless. I have a good friend with a photographic memory. It is the most phenomenal thing you can imagine. She can read a paragraph out of a technical manual for isotipic radiographic rocket science and repeat, an hour later, everything in that paragraph word for word. She cannot, however, walk and chew gum at the same time. Go figure.

Now what has been bugging me for all these years is this little book, illustrated by Dr. Seuss, titled *Pocket Book of Boners*. Now I know what you are thinking, but this was written in the early '30s and words sort of shift around a bit over the decades (if you don't believe me, Wiki it!). In it, was a section about science. In this science section was a bit about how Ben Franklin discovered electricity. Here is where my memory begins to fade. I can't remember if the book said that ol' Ben discovered electricity by rubbing two cats together or rubbing one cat backwards. If you happen to have that book, I would sure like to know the answer. Currently, I do not live in Albuquerque, New Mexico and cannot be found there. My oldest son, however, does live there and has the same name, so if you can get a hold of him, tell him the answer.

He will think you are a nut.

We are told by science that cats have been around for about as long as man has. God tells us that cats have been around since the day we were. We simply go back a long ways, toward the beginning.

Science also relates to us that cats still have bunches of repressed instinct left in them that is just raring to go primordial. Science informs us, the uninformed, that cats are always on the brink of taking just one little step backwards and into the wild. Science communicates to us that cats are not really domesticated animals like the llama and the goldfish, but deep down inside they are really ferocious hunters.

I don't know about you, but I've had a gozillion cats in my day and most of them were hairy tubs-o-lard that took up couch space. Indeed, if it weren't for the microseconds of antical behavior that they bring us, I'd say fire up the grill. Well, not really--no one in their right mind would eat a cat. However, I do hear that they taste like chicken.

Actually, it isn't so much that cats do things that amuse us, but they cause us to behave in ways that has to be amusing to them. I can still see my Grandmother, way up in her nineties, acting like a little girl while she tries to make the cat jump for the string. Bottom line is that you've gotta love cats.

Cat haters are a mystery to me, however, after a decade or so of counseling I believe I can at least grasp the *why* for those who go out of their way to harm or destroy a cat. Clinically, those folks are socially retarded idiots who are disfunkshinal in two or more areas of their lives to the point of being mentally and emotionally disabled. Nuff said.

I've seen grown men of the burly order be zonkered by a cat. You know the type: barrel chested he-men who would rather be run over by a train than watch a chic flick. Men who haven't shed a tear ever in their lives and would as soon take a whoopin' with a baseball bat rather than become remotely sentimental about something or anything! Now, put a cat in front of them. Better yet, a kitten. Watch what happens. Nuff said.

I like cats, contrary to what some people say. I like them, but tend to look at them very pragmatically and in a utilitarian vein. In other words, I hate to spend money on an animal that I don't/*can't* spend on myself. Certainly wouldn't want to take from the wife and kids and place in the hands of any animal. Just simply doesn't make sense and isn't right. However, there was this one cat.

Actually, it began with a whole string of cats and my dear wife back when we were first united in holy matrimony. There we were, stranded socially in the high plains of Southeastern New Mexico, so I decided to get her a cat. A cute little kitten. She loved it to death and would sit for hours cooing and cottling this kitten. Now in her line of work, she was always in danger of having to leave town for a day or two. She got one of those calls. She left, and so did the cat.

Now, mind you, I haven't to this day got so much as a clue as to what happened to that cat. It was there, then it wasn't. I fed it lunch, I'm sure, then it just disappeared into thin air. I called it, I walked around the house and banged the bowl. I jingled the sack of dry food. I sat out in the driveway in the Lotus position with an opened can of cat food. I pretended to eat the cat food. I left the front door open. I left the back door open. I looked in the clothes dryer. That cat was gone. To this day, my story isn't believed.

So, I did what any self-preserving husband would do--I went out and got another cat to replace it. That doesn't work with some things. Ruin your wife's good sweater and don't even try to go buy another one. Accidentally break some wedding china and you will roast in Hell for eternity, for replacing doesn't count. But with cats and other small furry mammals, it seems to work. I did it. I got one.

And as soon as I got this cat, she melted, became attached

to it and gave it a name. She would play with it and let it sleep in her lap in the evenings by the fire. She would buy it special catnip dinner type treats and toys. She would run through the house chasing the cat, then on the next trip being chased by the cat. At night, the cat was between us as we lay asleep under a blanket on a winter night. Sorry, I can't go on in this direction. Get the picture?

By and by the phone rang and she had to find herself out of town for a day or two. The day wore on and I was OK there alone, just me and the cat and the mortgage. Then it is supper time. The cat didn't come.

Now, this is just too real and too eerie to be totally true. I hunted for the cat. I called for the cat. I looked and looked and looked. You know the type of looking I'm talking about. The irrational looking that has you looking *everywhere* for something. I looked in the icebox, the silverware drawer, under the bathroom scales, the tread of the truck tires, everywhere! "I Gotta No Gato," as we would say in español. I held a vigil all night. I sat under the stars calling, "kitty, kitty, kitty," but to no avail. I even found myself looking upward into the stars as if the silly thing was airlifted by aliens or something. The darn thing was just gone, that's all there is! Again--and I might say this emphatically--to this day my story just simply   isn't believed.

You know where this is already going. The first cat can be tossed off as a fluke. It just happened to be that cat's time when she was out of town. It just happened to sort of disappear. It was just a once in a lifetime thing like winning a $10 scratch-off at the grocery store or a meteor hitting your house. However, no matter how much of a minor miracle the second cat is; no matter the odds; no matter that the odds are less than Vegas, she ain't gonna believe it one bit. Somehow I'm to blame in the cat's disappearance and assumed demise!

I begged, I pleaded, I groveled. Hey, guys, this is *early* in the marriage before groveling is second nature. Then I got another cat.

She didn't warm up to this cat as quickly as the first. I got it just after lunch and it was near supper time before they were best of friends. The cat's name was Blatz, which isn't so strange since all my cat's names were Blatz since as far back as I can remember. Actually, I rescued a kitten off the hot freeway in Texas in the summertime and that was Blatz One. Little paws pads were burned, but other than that, OK. Now, Blatz VI. Blatz IV & V were sort of short lived, as you have been informed. The phone rang again. She had to go out of town. You guessed it, the cat wandered off. I'm still dumbfounded to this day.

I sat on the back porch in the failing desert sunlight, wondering if I should hire a fellow I knew named Guido to come break my legs and torch the house. In the long run, it would have been worth it. Much, I assumed, could be attributed to it. It is about the time I seriously considered reaching for the phone, that I heard a 'meow' and a cat scratching at the back fence. Aha, safe!

I opened the gate to reveal a rather disheveled looking kitten. It was my kitten (or her kitten, rather), but it was walking funny. It would sort of drag its little back legs as it pulled itself along in pain across the grass. I grabbed it and flipped it over (which is, incidentally, how you tell a boy cat from a girl cat) but could find nothing wrong with it. Tummy a little swollen but other than...wait! Hold the bus. What was I thinking?! The cat was dying right in front of my eyes. I called the vet.

The vet was working a bit later than usual. She decided to worm some sheep or whatever vets do when it gets late. My frantic call on the answering machine piqued her interest. Would I be interested in bringing the cat in first thing in the morning?

Absolutely not! I'm heading her way right now. However, she balks at the idea. I did find out that vets can be persuaded with two approaches: 1) I boldly state that money is no object, and 2) I knew a fellow named Guido who had a bat, gasoline and matches. That and my charm (not to mention my good looks) got me a chance to see the doctor that night with this little sick, dying kitten.

Now, when I said that money was no object I didn't quite have in mind the $600 that it cost me to keep this cat alive. It had broken bones and bent spleens and infections in places and parts that most mammals don't have. It was anemic and jaundiced and, therefore, needed optimizing, simonizing and martinizing for good measure. It had more bandages on it when we left the animal hospital than were ever passed out at Gettysburg. But it was alive, and that is what mattered. You men know good and well what was at stake here.

Before you judge me too heavily (guys), or make me out to be some sort of softie (girls), it is purely a survival thing. Think of the alternative and the aftermath had I been forced to pronounce the arrival of Blatz VII. I would have lived--but just barely, and it would have been ugly.

Now for the pragmatic tug of war that I have fought several times in our married life. Now that $600 has been sunk into this feline, what does one do now? Six hundred bucks is a chunk of change (and was even more so nearly 20 years ago), but do you stop there, or call it the beginning of an investment? I opted for the latter, thanking my lucky stars every day that this silly cat didn't die on me. I do not believe in lucky stars, horrorscopes or any other astrological stuff. However, when one is stressed out to the max and your whole life hinges on something--one will resort to anything.

Bunches of moons later, this cat is still hanging around. It turned out to be one of the smartest cats I have ever had, even knowing that it seemed to have the upper hand when it came to my wallet. This cat would purposefully torment me by walking into the middle of the room, grab my attention with a mournful kitty wail, fall down and start convulsing complete with spasms and foaming at the whiskers. Just about the time that I would grab my wallet and my keys to the truck, the cat would get up, stretch, lick a paw or two, then walk away with this sheep eatin' grin on its face. It knew full well what it was doing.

I secretly hated that cat.

As smart as Blatz VI was, Psycho I, who inevitably came later, was way in the other direction. In fact, it was so stupid so early on, that we discontinued the Blatz line in favor of a more descriptive nomenclature. Why do we feel the need for a cat on a continuous basis? Same unidentifiable reason that everyone else comes up with. You have a cat, and wish you didn't have a cat. You say things like, "This is absolutely the last pet we're ever gonna have! I'm tired of the hair/smell/work/litterbox (you throw them in how ever you want). Then, you won't have a cat around and someone will say at the dinner table, "Why don't we have a cat?" It won't be so much an information gathering question as a statement. Others will muse it over and then, within a day, a cat will appear from wherever cats appear from. And these won't be fancy pug nosed, long haired, Persian show cats. These will just be the regular old fashioned, striped, hard tailed cat. And so was Psycho I.

My wife bonded with this unfortunate animal like she did countless times before, however, that particular animal-human bonding was to be short lived. One evening she scolded the Psycho Cat for being up on the dining room table, whereupon the cat slinked off the table and into a dining chair. After she got her way with this small animal, my dear wife retired to the living room to read a book. I joined her, but wasn't so much reading as I was watching this psychotic cat watch her.

Psycho began to intently watch and switch her tail. The same kind of intent switching that a normal, regular cat will do before attacking such things as houseflies and moths (remember, these are beasts that are one step away from the wild). Soon, when the psychotic beast could stand it no more, she sprang into action. The cat leapt from the chair and ran across the open expanse of the dining room and into the sitting room. Up one side of the couch she ran and across the back, running the length of it. Midair flight ended with the landing on the second of the pit group that my wife happened to be sitting on. Across the back of that couch the beast lumbered and finally lunged and swiped the side of my wife's face with a deadly clawing action. Not wishing to hang around and enjoy the consequences, the cat flew from the couch and rocketed down the hall. Hmm, who said that animals don't hold grudges?

I knew better than to laugh. You married men know full well what I mean. There are times when things are funny--just funny. But it ranked right up there with the loaded question of "How do I look in this...?" Sure, it might make her butt stand out a little more. Might be a little tight in the waist--which has grown a bit over the years for every wife. Might just be downright ridiculous looking---but better to keep your mouth shut in times like that.

I also knew better than to join her on what has come to be called in our family the Great Cat Hunt of 1996. All the time that mattresses where being flipped over and closets rifled, my dear spouse was describing very loudly just how worthless this cat was and in just what shape this cat would be in when she found it since it was a worthless-good-for-nothing-cat. However, that was not to be the case. I found, purely by accident, that cats can be very useful tools. Move over Bob Vila.

Time came to re-carpet. That time comes every so often. Now with the new carpet in, the vent grilles look like they need repainting. Can't have rusty vent grilles on new carpet. Just won't do. Besides, I'm kind of pretty handy sometimes with a few odds and ends around the old homestead, and I do believe that I can spray paint a grille.

So there we are, without any grilles in the forced air ducts. Being a hugely oversized, gigantic, two story colonial style house, the forced air vents were floor upstairs and ceiling below. Sort of a large octopus duct work type thing coming off of one central blower. All the little grilles were dutifully lining the driveway, recovering from a fresh coat of white paint. While standing in the living room, admiring what I had half completed at this point, I heard a faint cry of a cat. Maybe it was outside? I went to have a look.

Now, no one ever accused this cat of being smart. Sure, she could come in and out of her little kitty door in the back of the house, but would insist on meowing at the front door. I guess she decided that the back of the house was another dimension. So, I opened the door but no cat. I closed the door and went back to admiring a job half done when I heard a faint cat distress call. I strained my ears. I heard it again and checked the door again. No cat. I checked the hall closet. So dumb that she would get herself locked in there from time to time for hours or overnight. No cat. No gato.

At that moment, a most hideous sight appeared before my eyes, threatening to damage my delicate nature: a cat emerged from one of the uncovered vents, all covered with fuzz, dust and whatever else grows and collects in the ductworks of Colonial Virginia Homes. The Beast from the Nether World! As I picked the cat up, I suddenly realized that the ribbing in the ductwork probably prevented the cat from being able to back up, once she decided she was in a place she didn't want to be. I knew then what I had to do. You, dear reader, would do it too.

After holding the cat out the front door and vigorously shaking all the dust and fuzz off the cat, I simply walked across the room and placed the cat in another vent. Within an hour, all my ducts were clean.

When we left Virginia, we dropped the cat off at my parents' house. It is still alive and well and they *claim* that the cat isn't psycho, however, I have my doubts.

As far as the Ben Franklin thing, I'm leaning towards the single cat being rubbed backwards--bad idea all around. Rubbing one kitty forward is OK, but rubbing two cats together is called Discovering Stupidity. I currently do not *own* a cat. I am--drum roll, please--cat free! But then again, does anyone ever really own a cat?

Addendum: I now, once again, have *two* cats: Thing One and Thing Two. Thing One is a Tub-o-Lard and Thing Two brings me birds. Psycho I is still alive at eighteen years old. My parents, however, never used her for cleaning their ducts.

Maybe there should have been some Proverbs concerning cats. I'll ask my secretary.

Minister's Feet

How beautiful are the feet of those who bring glad tidings of good things! Romans 10:15

Try this next Sunday after morning worship: We all like to get out of the church building in a lightning flash on Sunday morning. Why? Well, it's simple. We must get to the buffet before the Methodists do (unless, of course, you *are* Methodist, in which case you are racing *everybody*!). Call it the Great Weekly Denominational Buffet Run. But make this next Sunday different. Time for an experiment.

Instead of shaking the Minister's hand and giving him the usual "Heidi-ho" and a big handshake on the way out the door (to the buffet), ask him to remove his shoes and socks. More than likely he will ask you why. Just say that you want to look at his feet and see what kind of feet he has.

He is either going to do one of two things. Your Preacher just might pull off his shoes and socks and sort of stick his foot out and wiggle his toes. At that point you are on your own. YOU will be responsible for something to say.

Or your Pastor will probably ask you to repeat your request. You will ask him again to remove his shoes so you can see what kind of feet he has. He will look at you sort of cockeyed and slowly shake his head from side to side in a NO fashion and then maybe try to talk to someone else. YOU will be responsible for something to say, both to the Minister and to those who heard you make the silly request in the first place!

Or, he might do a third thing and that is whack you on the nose with his Bible. So, keep a tissue handy.

Actually, this little item doesn't have anything at all to do with the Minister's feet. I just thought it was pretty catchy and would cause you to want to read it. Now that I have you unmovingly hooked, I do have a foot question which is: what is a pteropodium?

A pteropodium is the foot of a pteropod, of course. You know, those little specialized free swimming pelagic sea snails that, well, free swim all day out in the wild blue. I have no earthly idea what a pelagic sea snail does, or even what they might be interested in--except of course, pelagic sea snails of the opposite sex. Come to think of it, I don't even know what pelagic means, I just know that they have nothing but time on their hands out in the open sea. Actually, they don't have hands, just feet and lots of time and open water.

You, of course, might have even less of an interest in pelagic sea snails than I do. I would really hate to lose you at this point (or have you throw this book in the trash), so I will switch from pteropodiums to another type of podium.

What is a terrorpodium? It is a podium where week after week, Sunday sermon after Sunday sermon, nothing but bad news and drummed up repentance based on drummed up guilt are spewed forth. To be sure, conviction of sin and repentance are very much a Bible subject. Indeed, it is a turnstile in our response toward God, however, we never want to be like the church where week after week the minister preaches everyone into Hell and the brethren line up at the back to glad-hand him and say, "Preach, you really spanked us today! Thanks for the sermon!"

Uhuh.

Last time I looked, the minister isn't in the whoopin' business and the church building isn't a woodshed. "If you love me," Jesus said, "you will keep my commandments." Check out John 14, verses 15 and 21. After you have done that, check out Exodus 20:6 and Deuteronomy 5:10 and notice what the context is for those verses. It is the giving of the Big Ten! Love draws.

If presented well, love will draw folks; and repentance and sorrow will issue forth from recognizing our heretofore reaction to that love--sin! Do a study on love and you will find that it is always a draw toward God, whether it be Old or New

Testament. Actually, you will find that it is THE draw toward God. He extends John 3:16 toward us, and asks us to respond likewise toward Him and our brethren with First John 3:16.

I was forced this week to read a Family Circle magazine. Not my first choice, but better than staring at the flies on the ceiling. I found a study from the Cincinnati Children's Hospital Medical Center which stated that adolescents who ate with their families were less likely to be depressed or use drugs than those who didn't. These 'family eaters' were also found to have better relationships with their peers and were more motivated at school. Now at the risk of sounding sarcastic, I won't comment on the above--except did we really need a study to tell us that?!

And then Sunday comes and we march these well-adjusted, family eating, adolescents off to the church building and subject them to a half hour of someone banging the pulpit and telling everyone just how bad they are, how degraded they are, how hell-bound they are and they need to repent? That's a Terrorpodium!

How messed up is that? A family dinner where everyone is around the table laughing and telling stories and eating makes for well-adjusted children while taking them to a church building is messing them up? Again, how messed up is that?

I'm not proposing that a Sunday morning worship service ought to be a variety show. I'm not proposing that a Sunday morning worship service ought to be a time for the shallow thought for the day. Neither am I proposing that the Sunday morning worship service ought to be a pooling of ignorance where everyone sort of jumps up and tells whatever is on their minds without a moment's thought. What I am proposing is that the Sunday morning worship service ought to center around something from God's word that will encourage and build up and teach those disciples who long to live like God and for God.

And that message ought to center in and around the love of God.

And so here's the catch. You have an assignment to do two things. The first is, if you aren't having a time where everyone sits around the table and talks and passes food and laughs and tells stories, then you need to create that time. I know, I know, everyone is way busy and way stressed and way involved with this activity or that activity. I know that we have to be here and there and only have enough time to shove a starchy thingy in the microwave and grab a soda out of the icebox and our cellphones are ringing or dinging at us because someone texted us and we need to text them back right away...

I also know that we can grind to a complete halt in order to catch TV's latest talent hunt or the latest reality race across America or watch a show where someone slaps meals together in a restaurant or run a pawn shop. Just give it a try!

How many times in the Bible is eating a meal either the crux of the story or the very big, very evident background? Jesus ate with sinners. Jesus ate with enemies. Jesus ate with friends and apostles. Jesus eats with us each time we take communion. Jesus made food on a couple of occasions when it ran short so everyone could have a meal. The kingdom of God can be compared to a great banquet...

The second assignment is this: look hard and fast at what you are being fed on Sunday morning. If you are indeed being fed, then thank God and continue on, disregarding this little entry. Also, give the feeder a raise or at least give him and his family a gift certificate to a nice restaurant: feed for feed. If you are not being fed, or you are being yelled at and diminished each Sunday, switch feedlots. It ain't God's message that is stinging your ears each week. His is one of love.

We truly are what we eat.

A third of mankind was killed by these three plagues, by the fire and the smoke and the brimstone which proceeded out of their mouths.
Revelation 9:18

Hitchhikers

Hermanos míos, ¿de qué le sirve a uno alegar que tiene fe, si no tiene obras? ¿Acaso podrá salvarlo esa fe? **Santiago 2:14**

There are, perhaps, unimaginable atrocities that we as human beings can, and still do, commit on one another. As technology progresses and times change, so will the ways and means to carry out these acts. However, unless we were part of Germany's Final Solution of World War II, we cannot fully empathize--we can only look at the pictures and hear the stories. Unless we witnessed what has come to be called the Rape of Nanking, we can only read the accounts and try to (or try not to) imagine the hell on earth that it must have been for literally thousands of Chinese at the hands of Imperial Japan. Unless we were living in the Deep South of the United States in the 1950's and early 1960's, whether we were black or white, again, we can only hear the tales and witness the video clips of beatings and humiliations with fire hoses turned full blast into crowds. However, not wanting to take anything from the aforementioned, the most humiliating may not be the most widespread or the most physical in its makeup. It simply may consist of a loss of dignity. Consider two people in Arizona.

Having just driven through Page, Arizona toward my final destination of Albuquerque, New Mexico, I entered a lonely stretch of blacktop that traversed the Navajo Nations. Now, this particular hundred or so mile stretch of blacktop certainly isn't the most desolate in North America. That distinction probably goes to the Boom and Bust state of Nevada. However, lonely is lonely and I needed it that way. No cars coming and no cars going. The weather was hot, but a promise of a downpour was visible on the horizon. Anyone who has grown up and hung out in cities all their life will find it hard to imagine that much of the western United States is still in this condition. No shopping mall, no Starbucks, no music store. Only nature at her severest, and nothing that we can do will ever change it.

I needed this stretch of road. I was running away. Not the kind of running away every kid dreams of at least once in their life from mean parents, but the adult version. I wasn't running away from my wife. Would never do that. Wasn't running away from my family or my responsibilities. Would never do that. Was running from a desperation that grips one when he realizes that his life's ambition and goal in life has died on the vine.

I was a Minister. A Preacher. Some called me a Pastor and sometimes Reverend. Either way, I had dedicated a large part of my life in trying to tie Heaven and earth together in my neck of the woods--wherever that was at the time. I had tried, retried and bent myself trying to change people to reflect, even if in some small way, God to others around them. I had been largely ignored, dismissed, patted on the head and on the back. I, and my family, had suffered retribution at the hands of those who had realized the Beast in their life through my teaching and instead of changing, had lashed out. I had found a lonely road, and was hoping that somehow this road would have no end.

Now in this country one can see for miles. Not just two or three, but for miles and miles. Fifty? Maybe a hundred. No one behind me and a truck in front of me that I was allowing a good mile lead or better to keep the sense of seclusion alive. I was wondering where I would pull over and sit out the night. I also was aware of two figures standing or walking along the side of this road to nowhere. This especially caught my attention when the truck in front of me momentarily put on its brake lights. It was at that point that the two figures along the edge of the road began to move further off the roadside. The truck spun its tires and moved on.

As I approached, I had dropped my speed. Caution, perhaps, but more out of a sense of interest. These two figurines began to take on a bit of identity. First, I could tell that it was a man and a woman. Next I could tell that they were up in years. Up in years to a 22 year old is someone who is 45. I was about 45, so someone who is up in years would be about 70. Ten years from now I'm sure I'll change my mind.

A Minister's Musing...in Shorts!

I couldn't for the life of me understand what this couple was doing out here in the middle of Arizona, she in a dress and he in dress pants and the temperature near 100. I hadn't passed any abandoned vehicles--that, I would have clearly remembered. I did know one thing, no two: It was about to rain, and rain hard and no two human beings needed to be out here with the promise of nothing in any direction for many, many miles.

I've been told not to pick up hitchhikers. I've even emphatically told others never to do the same. I've also been brought up to believe that passing someone by in need is no better than the Priest or Levite in the story of the Good Samaritan in the Gospel of Luke. No matter what their reason (they had none) or their excuse (I'm sure they had several), Jesus said that they were just wrong, pure and simple. They made the wrong choice. Again, I had no clue as to why this older couple was out here. It didn't matter why. People end up in strange and unpredictable circumstances all the time and must rely on other people to assist them out of the particular situation. I pulled over. They cautiously approached my truck.

Did I mention that they were Navajos? I don't need to, other than it does figure heavily into my story. I'm not so naive as to buy into this fandango of 'oneness' that so many preach and teach. Our cultures and our racial heritage make us different. Wake up! We have black people on earth. We have white people on earth. We have brown people on earth. We have spokidotted people on earth. Look hard enough and we might find a race of light green folks somewhere in Antarctica. We have people who build One Nation Under God. Some build one nation under Allah. Some worship Father Sky, Mother Earth and Brother Beaver. Some hold one thing in high regard while others disdain it. Political ideologies and tongues further separate us.

However, the bottom line is that people are people and should be treated with the same amount of dignity no matter the color of their skin or their ideologies. There is a base line of human dignity that we ought not rob one another of, no matter what the conflict. Rob a man of his wallet, and he can someday replace it. Rob him of his dignity, and he will be a long time regaining it--or never. It can never be paid back, even from the one who did the robbing. I soon found out that this couple had just had their dignity ripped from them on the side of the road on a hot afternoon in Arizona.

Who were they? Just an old couple. Just a couple of Navajos on the side of the road without a car. Just another pair of hitchhikers looking for a free ride. But let's look deeper.

I had to gain my story from her. He couldn't speak English and I couldn't speak any Diné. As the story unfolded, they had one son who was born with severe mental problems. Not a handicap problem that is taken care of with special parking privileges, extra wide doors and ramps, but insurmountable problems. The kind of life that can't be lived without the assistance of others. He had been institutionalized all his 28 year life in a special facility in Tuba City. Each weekend, for God knows how long, this old couple had faithfully hitchhiked from their home to the special facility in Tuba City to visit their unresponsive son. Sometimes this eighty-five mile one way trip took all day each way--and into the next, or the next. Sometimes they slept along the side of the road when the night sky was black and moonless. When snow covered the ground, it gave them enough light to walk all night. Their greatest fear was that soon they would be too old to both make the trip each week. Then who would visit their son? Who would go to Tuba City each week and tell him that he was someone special, even though all things, and a fast paced society, pointed to the fact that he was not?

Seems also that the favorite past time of some is to pick up hitchhikers--especially Indians--then dump them when they are the farthest from any point of civilization, laughing when they drove off. Some, like the truck in front of me, would throw something out the window at them. She showed me the mayonnaise from his half eaten sandwich-turned-projectile still on her dress. She reached into one of her pockets for a handkerchief, wiped her dress with all the feminine dignity that she had left, then quickly fixed her hair in my rearview mirror. He was sound asleep from the moment he shut the door of the truck.

She talked of herding sheep and cleaning houses. She talked of her husband working hard for a living and not allowing himself to be sucked under by alcohol like all of his brothers and hers. She talked of a fire that burned their hogan many years ago and a sickness that killed all their goats one summer. She talked of their relationship with Jesus Christ. She talked about one day being in Heaven with her son and being able to converse with him the way she has always wanted to do. She longed to hear her son say just one simple phrase, "Mother, I love you." She asked me what I did for a living. I was hesitant, no, reluctant to say.

As we topped the next hill, she said that this was their place and that I could let them out on the side of the road. I saw no place, only an unmarked dirt road leading back into nowhere.

They were delivered to their door, about two miles back into the dusty woods. A few skinny dogs came out to greet us, barking at the unfamiliar truck. There was no green lawn or any patio furniture under a shade tree. Feed sacks stood in for curtains. I saw a pole, but no electrical line feeding the house. I did see a hand pump at the side of the house. They apologized for living at the standard that they did.

I have preached many sermons over the past years on Luke chapter 10 and the Good Samaritan. I have tried, mostly in vain, to rally a group of folks together to imitate Jesus. My sermons, I fear, have fallen on ears that are connected to heads that are more concerned in life with skidoos, travel trailers and bigger hard drives. My homilies have been delivered on Sunday mornings. By Sunday afternoons, the recipients have been more concerned with Sunday lunch than Sunday sermon. In despair, I have fled the pulpit trying to figure out just what God had in mind for me in this life. I spent the previous few days camping and driving alone in desolation, spending my days staring out of a windshield at vastness and spending my nights staring into a campfire wondering what it was all about.

As they left my truck for home, the man shook my hand. Even though we couldn't communicate verbally with each other I knew all too well what his handshake was all about. Call it a man thing if you will. It was the shake that was appreciative on the one hand, but on the other hand spoke of sadness that once again he and his wife were at the mercy of another. She hugged my neck and gave me her address and asked me to write them when I got my family to New Mexico to start another life.

She left with the words, "God bless you." Not in the way that someone would in a simple salutation or closure, but in a way that genuinely told me that what I had done had partially made up for both the abandonment along Highway Nowhere and the half eaten sandwich. I wondered if the man who had given them the first ride under false pretenses, dumping them far from anywhere in the blistering heat would have second thoughts about it that evening when he faced his wife and children across from the dinner table. I wondered what Sandwich Man would think that night before he went to sleep. I wondered what next Sunday's sermon would be about from the pulpit that for four and a half years I called home. I wondered what response it would bring from the listeners after they patted the speaker on the back and told him what a wonderful job he did with the day's lesson.

I drove away with dogs barking at my truck. The old couple lit a lamp and set it in the window. Somewhere in Tuba City a nurse was once again changing bed sheets and wiping drool off a human being that we have yet as a society decided what to do with.

Driving down the dirt road out of sight from their house, I stopped. I pretended to get out to stretch my legs a bit. I looked upward at the reddening sky to reassure myself that God was still on His throne and that the sun would once again come up on the morrow. It's hard not to cry in times like these.

She Liked Fudge!

I was sick, and you visited me.
Jeshua barJoseph

I remember the story of the preacher who was asked to do a funeral service for someone he had never met. To the best of my knowledge, this story came from John Gipson, a gospel preacher in Little Rock, Arkansas. He met with the family an hour before the actual memorial began. When the family gathered, he began to ask about some special memories, some event or some quality that they would want to share with the small group that was beginning to gather in the funeral parlor. Silence was followed by more silence. The preacher reworded his request, allowing the family--the people who knew her best--to gather their thoughts. Finally, one fellow spoke up and said, "She liked fudge." That was it: *she liked fudge!* That was the sum total of the good qualities and a life lived here on earth. It spoke more of a wasted, self-centered and self-deluded life than anything else.

In another memorial service, both a Priest and a Minister were asked to officiate. The body had been cremated in death. In life, the man was a monster. He had terrorized and ruined his children. He had driven the children's mother to the point of insanity. He had been physical, mental and emotional in his abuse of everyone. Now, the family wanted to somehow have gracious words said over his ashes. One family member showed up. Folks scooted and adjusted to give him room to sit at the table.

He declined to sit, however, he lifted the lid to the urn, doodled his finger in the ashes, replaced the lid and began to depart. When asked if he was indeed leaving, the man rather cooly stated that, indeed, he was. He also added, "I just wanted to make sure that the S.O.B. was really dead!"

We will not, for the most part, *wow* the world. Most of us will pass without anyone sculpting a bronze statue of us. Actually, statues and our individual names will probably never come up together in the same sentence. We will not have a wing of a building dedicated to us and bear our name. Parks, streets, bridges and districts will not bear our name, either. We will survive a few decades in the minds of family and in photo albums. A few decades past that, and we will be a simple fill-in-the-blank on a genealogy hunt. What matters is how we prepare for eternity, after our brief threescore and ten. Eternity is a long time, but is set by our life here on earth and the choices that we make. How 'bout it? What will we say about you when that time comes?

Time is spent on wondering (daydreaming) about what kind of impact that we will have well into decades past us. That is simply the wrong question, which needs to be rephrased into what kind of impact we are having *now* on the people around us. Are we truthful? Many today aren't, even in everyday conversation. Are we trustworthy? Many today aren't, even in the little things like promised secrets to keep. Are we loyal? Many today aren't, sitting on fences waiting for the shifting of the tides. Are we helpful? Many today aren't, centering more on opportunity than sacrifice. I'll stop, before I go through the entire Boy Scout Law.

Though not dying--or even remotely close to it--I just got off of the phone with a lady who was in the hospital over in the next town. Part of the duty of the minister is to go see everyone that I possibly can who has had surgery or is in the hospital for any other reason. Woe be unto the minister that fails to visit someone in the hospital. Been there and received that…

People are funny. There are people who have elective day surgery and do not wish to tell anyone that they are "going in and going under" for one reason or another. Maybe they don't want to be seen with their makeup off. Maybe they are not too overjoyed at the prospects of the whole world seeing them in one of those little hospital gowns. You know, try as you might, you're just going to end up mooning and squirreling the world sometime or another in one of those things. Wear something like that in public out on the street and you will be arrested immediately. Try *not* to wear one of those things in a hospital

A Minister's Musing...in Shorts!

and you will be arrested by hospital security for not being a team player. Anyway, back to funny people.

Take the woman who will remain nameless. She had one of those in-by-6am-out-by-2pm surgeries. She told no one. She drove herself to the hospital and then back home. She recouped at home for a few days, which included Sunday. Missing her on Sunday, I called her that following Monday to see what the score was. I promptly got chewed for not visiting her in the hospital, and then not coming by to wish her well while she recuperated at home. Go figure. All I can tell that was missing from my formal preacher training was telepathy.

Anyway, I'm talking to this lady who just had a bunch of stuff removed from inside the main body cavity. I'm always suspicious of all those bags of cedar shavings that are shipped to the hospitals around the country. Do they fill in the blank spots with wood chips? I called the main number for the hospital and got the switchboard operator, who asked me the same question that I always get.

"Hello, thank you for calling Good Sam Hospital. How may I direct your call?"

Now I'm a big fan of saying please and thank you, but I wonder why she is thanking me for calling this particular hospital. I don't have a choice. The woman I want to speak to is in there, somewhere! I decide to go on and bypass that one. "Yes, I would like to speak to a patient named Thelma K__ I don't know her room number."

"What room is she in, please?"

Now, I'm banking on the fact that this lady was not listening to me. Perhaps she is reading from a script or something. However, the fact still stands that I do not under any circumstances know what room this girl is in. I know she is in there, but I'm having to fall on the mercy seat held by this switchboard operator, hoping like all get out that she will somehow be able to find my friend in a database somewhere---somehow. "I don't know her room number, ma'am." Ma'am can't hurt at this point, I believe.

"What is the patient's name?"

Now I know for a fact that she isn't listening at this point. Notice that the question is even genderless. However, while I've got her on the line, I decide to have some fun at this point.

I'll just bet, too, on the fact that her database will be listed by last name. "Her name is Thelma."

"Does Thelma have a last name?" I'm asked.

"No, she doesn't," I want to say. "There are, perhaps, 6 billion people on the planet...or is that 6 billion Chinese? People are born and die every second of every day and we are but a mere drop in the bucket of humanity. No two people look alike. No one shares fingerprints with another human being past, present or future. The list goes on, but out of these billions and billions of folks, Thelma is the only one without a last name. Astounding!" ...but I decide to drop it and give the operator the last name.

"Just a moment."

Now at this particular place in all of this banter, it would be a really, really good thing to share the room number and phone info with me in case I, or someone close to me, decides to call back. But the phone rings straight through to my disemboweled friend, and I decide it is a power thing with the operator.

We chat about the weather and the operation. She tells me what they removed and I tell her of all the people that I know that died from this type of operation. She tells me what she ate and I tell her that she will be glad to get out of there. Being a little groggy at this point (Thelma, not me), I begin to wind down the conversation. I ask her what room she is in, because I may come up and see her (but I really want to know just because the switchboard operator wouldn't privy me on that one). She didn't know. Guess she didn't need to know. Not like she was going to be allowed to walk around and get lost or something and then be one of those eternal patients who are destined to walk the halls of the hospital, butt hanging out and eating the leftovers from food trays that they manage to commandeer by ambushing them as they got off the elevator.

"Look out the window from your bed and estimate how many floors up you are and which side of the building you are on."

"I would have to get out of bed to do that. I can't see the window from here."

"Look on your wristband and see what room number you are in."

"I don't have my glasses on."

At this point we part and I hang up a frustrated person. I do not know where she is, other than in the hospital over in the next town.

Life is like that. We have so many questions and we constantly run into people who hold the answers to those questions and try as we might we cannot pry those answers out of people's mouths. We get angry and have to hold it in, knowing that not holding the answer to that particular question will just mean that we will have to ask the question again and may have to *gag* ask the *same person* the question which will be humiliating. Advice? There is none. It is just one of those things that happens. That is the end of the story.

A very small percentage of readers at this point may be asking themselves just how this story can start out talking about a very vile man who was cremated and a self-centered woman who can only be remembered by the fact that she liked fudge, hang a left turn on a hospital phone call and end up here? Rest assured that you are not alone. I, too, am one of those people who have that very same question and as of yet, I do not have the answer I so desperately seek.

In the meantime, however, while we continue to look for an answer, if you are ever in a hospital and find yourself suddenly surrounded by gaunt, pale stick figures wearing backless gowns and no shoes, know that they do not mean to harm you. They are only hungry.

Buy them some fudge from the vending machine.

For I was hungry, and you gave Me something to eat; naked, and you clothed Me. Jesus

TechnoWorship

And all the people gathered as one man...Then Ezra the priest...read from the Law...from early morning until midday...and all the people were attentive. **Nehemiah 8:1*ff***

I like technology. My computer is essential and my cellphone is in itself fast becoming essential, also. I don't know a whole lot about my cellphone. If something goes wrong with it, or I try to figure out something about my cellphone, someone (usually a LOT younger than me) simply takes it away from me, fixes it, hands it back to me and says, "OK, now it will do that thing you wanted." Therefore, I am no smarter than when I first perceived a problem.

There was a time when I dismissed cellphones as senseless toys for teens. That was until I found myself at a car wash with no keys. I had keys up to a point, but after vacuuming out the car I had none. Now I know I got there somehow in my car, but now the keys were nowhere to be found.

And I had left my cellphone at home.

There is something about having to ask a total stranger for help that rubs me the wrong way. It's a little like asking for directions. Not that actually having to bow and ask for help is the great equalizer, but knowing just how the conversation would go:

I start, "Um, excuse me. Do you work here?"

"Well, since I'm going from wash bay to wash bay cleaning up, and carrying this bucket and broom around, I'd say it's a pretty good bet that I belong here. Having trouble with one of the vacuums or car wands?"

"Well, no. I seem to have lost my keys somewhere between

the time I drove up to the time I finished cleaning out the inside of the car."

"Oh, no problem. I'll open up the vacuum trap and get them out for you." He does, but there doesn't seem to be any keys amongst all the stuff that got sucked out of people's cars. I saw loose change--big stuff like quarters--and instinctively wanted to grab some. I figured he must do that at the end of the day, for he saw me spying some out and slammed the door. "Well, don't know what to tell you, Buddy."

About this time the owner was joined by his wife who had been doing whatever car wash spouses do around the facility, but had to come over and see what was happening. Perhaps she could smell something brewing. She said, "What are you two discussing over here?"

"Well, this fellow lost his keys. I've already checked the sweeper trap."

"Did you have them with you when you got here?" Then she caught herself and followed with, "Well, guess you had to have them to drive, didn't you?" People do that from time to time. It's a technique called Autodoof Reversing. We probably don't do it often enough.

Now, as it turned out I had inadvertently thrown them away with some other trash that was quickly gathered up from the vehicle before dropping in a wad of quarters to start the high speed dirt sucker. Yes, it did turn out that way but not for a little while, or a long while. I knew I had to ask to borrow their phone.

"Would it be too much trouble to borrow a phone so I can call my wife to bail me out yet one more time in my little miserable life?"

In unison: "Did you lose your cellphone, too!?"

"No, I accidentally LEFT IT AT HOME."

One didn't speak, only shook their head. The other simply asked, "Why?"

So it is inevitable. Something comes along and sooner or later it becomes a necessity. I can still remember party lines. I can still remember person to person long distance. I can still remember a long distance operator. I'm just sure that there were some folks back then that insisted that a phone hardwired into one's house just wasn't a necessity but a luxury. Their reasoning was that if someone really wanted to get in touch with you they could send a letter and it would put you in the know in less than a week. Case closed. I wonder how folks used to call in sick before phones?

No, I really want to know. Y'know what I just did? I texted my 102 year old Grandmother and asked her. I got my answer, so allow me to digress just a little bit. Way back when (on the subject of calling in sick), one simply didn't get sick. If you couldn't make it to work it was because BOTH legs were missing and you couldn't get up onto your horse or walk to work. In this worst case scenario, a family member either walked or rode their own horse (or yours--remember, you're sick :-) to your place of employment and notified the boss.

No, my Grandmother didn't text me back. I got a callback (on a cellphone) and we had one of those family pass the phone thingies. So here I have my 102 year old Grandmother, my 80 year old Mother and my way-older-than-me sister passing the cell. Somewhere in there my Mother asked my Grandmother about their first phone. My mother remembers it being in the early years of the Great Depression--a huge, cast iron two-handed phone mounted with bolts on the wall in the hall. Conversation went something like this (Remember, everyone is yelling 'cause no one can hear!):

"Mama," my Mother hollered towards my Grandmother, "Do you remember that big ol' phone that was hanging in the wall of that first house?"

My Grandmother hollered back, "Why, sure, I remember that phone. Why?"

"Well," Mama mused loudly, "I was wondering what we mainly used it for."

"Well," Grandmother straight faced back, "I believe it was mostly for phone calls!"

And so, there you go! A hundred and two years young and still tossin' them out.

Anyway, back to the inevitable. Computers come along and become a necessity. The internet comes along, dragging e-mail with it, and becomes a necessity. Even billboards have changed from paper plastered plywood to multi-changing small GIFF's dancing before your eyes as you creep through traffic, cursing the other drivers. And there is always a cellphone. Not even just a phone anymore. A calendar, alarm clock, DJ, mobile e-mail center and a host of other items that I'm sure I'm missing. I should have consulted my grown children while writing this section.

Technology has found its way into the church, also. Actually, I should say the church building. Sure, disciples are running around with their noses buried in their cells but I mean the church building, especially on Sunday morning during worship.

I've watched this slowly become incorporated into the Sunday morning lineup over the years. I have concerns about this matter. Now, I know what some of you might want to say at this point: "Oh, brother! Hang on while he rants and raves about the church needing to be tight, rote and very un-thrilling." But, no, I'm not for tight, rote and no thrill anything on Sunday morning. Allow me a little lecture time here.

We have things we all believe need to be carried out on Sunday morning. The group I was closely associated with for many years had five things. These were listed as a must each and every Sunday: giving, singing, praying, communion and a sermon. Other groups had their lists, and still do. The problem with technology is that it has added another item to the Sunday morning musts.

I'm not yet sure what to call this new item. For a while there I called it entertainment, but while that seems to fit on the surface, it doesn't fit when closely examined, or does it? I'm not even sure that it is an entity unto itself, since in reality and practice it is throughout all of the many things we do on a Sunday morning. Let's go back over the list that I gave for my neck of the woods. The first is giving. Why am I listing this first? Simply because money makes the world go round. A church might have to change around a bit on Sunday morning due to unforeseen circumstances, but they will always seem to find time to pass the plate!

In order to collect, there must be some sort of systematic way that money goes from all of the individuals into a central coffer with a minimum of fuss and regret. Most religious outfits have pretty much resorted to passing plates. Maybe everyone, or a choir, sang while these plates were passed, but that was usually because we can't stand all of that silence when we are departing with our hard earned cash. Too much like a funeral for money. Nowadays, we have to have pictures or short movies projected on the screens of starving children somewhere in Africa or South America. Little brown skinned, potbellied children with flies around their mouths as they stand in ankle deep sewage in the middle of ramshackle squalor.

Truth be known, and I say this as one who knows the ropes--and knows them well--that about eighty five cents out of every dollar collected will go to pay for the church building, the paid staff and all of that audio/visual equipment that is streaming those movies and images before our eyes each Sunday.

Singing is next. I want to know what has happened to my song book? That is the little book that had a collection of hymns in it, but also contained the notes for the song that tells me how that song is to be sung! Now I realize that the majority of people do not read music. Of those who do read music, many of those do not know how to translate it into singing (as opposed to piano keys or notes blown on a tuba). In other words, sight reading for voice is a rarity--but not totally unheard of. One thing is for sure, everyone at least knows that if the particular note they're singing is in-between the bottom and the next to the bottom line and the next note is moved up a notch, then their voice is going to have to move up a notch the next time.

If all I'm given are the words splashed up on the big screen in letters nine inches tall, how do I know what to do with them? Is it a fast song? Is it in a minor key? Are there any holds or crescendos? I'm left with having to hear the song forty five times before I can join in--then it is an old song and we won't sing it any more. Time would fail me if I continued to talk about technology and communion, or technology and prayers. Time would not only fail me, but would probably end if I took up the subject of technology and sermons!

But what do we really come together for on a Sunday morning? What is, or should be, our main purpose and goal? Is it, as we have been told, really a time to be a soul filling station? Is it really a time for praise and worship (read: spiffy choirs and snappy tunes)? In fact, what it really boils down to is a time to look into God's will for mankind and build ourselves up with it and through it.

I'm talking about Bible study and Bible learning. Yes, I'm well aware of passages like First Corinthians 14:26, Ephesians 5:19 and Colossians 3:16. They mention singing, yes, but they also mention other things that we just don't do when we get together. We've turned too much of our precious time over on Sunday morning to singing or being sung to while flies continue to buzz around a small dark child.

Or entertained?

I've heard the entertainment argument for decades. I came from a non-choir, non-musical instrument (read: piano/band) group that would rather sing a cappella than take a chance on getting God all tiffed and going to Hell. It was easy to look at all those great sounding choirs, very melodic keyboard tunes, and great sounding bands and place the entertainment stamp on it. Believe me, it was VERY easy to place the entertainment stamp on lousy choirs, bad bands and Liberace wannabes.

But seems as if even we were destined to fall to the entertainment monkey. Now we don't technically have choirs, we have praise teams. They don't officially stand on the stage, but sit out in the auditorium (we don't have sanctuaries, either) so God wouldn't see them and mistake them for a choir and get tiffed. We gave them microphones and they sing all the parts--soprano, alto, tenor, bass--just like the first century church did, while under the direction of the song leader who is allowed to stand up in front of us and sort of dance in place because he's what the Bible calls an expedient. I'm having trouble finding the expedient verse right now but when I do I will include it in further printings.

We also pull in the technology monkey, full swing, into our singing time. We never seem to get far enough away from the technosimian before he comes swinging back into our Sunday morning. Now, we have slide shows of mountains and streams and starving children with mouth flies while we are singing and forget the song books because we have words tall enough to wear as a shirt. The lights are dimmed to help us focus on God and a few folks hold up their hands because the song leader has his hands up and he doesn't have a clue why except he saw kids do it at a youth rally and he's afraid of getting old and when a certain part of the song comes by everyone stands up and begins to clap.

We're entertaining ourselves.

God tells us that the purpose for singing is edification. That word speaks of building up through instruction. That word doesn't say anything about goose bumps. Why does God want his people to be built up? Same reason Paul told Timothy to pay close attention to himself and to his teaching. Why? So that Timothy could assure salvation for himself and for those who Timothy taught.

The Devil will be staved if we have the word of God in our brains and in our lives. In other words when the temptation to do such and such comes along and I know that in Haggaliah 3:18 there is a clear passage that states that God is displeased with such and such, then I will tell the Devil that I'm not going to do such and such.

If all I have is the memory of a tingly song where we get to all jump up and raise our hands together at this certain part of the song where the worship leader holds his hands up high and the lights are dimmed and thousands of starving fly mouthed children come streaming onto the big screen as we get goose bumps big enough to hang our hats on...then I will say to Satan, "Sure, let's go do such and such. I'll buy!"

I'm in the process of moving from one city to another in another state. We will spend considerable time visiting religious outfits for many Sundays. One of the items that we will look for is the depth of teaching. Even church web sites hold out their technology and tinglies, and hardly say anything about their depth of teaching. That's if you can get them to say anything about it at all.

Info hunting on teaching is a little like info hunting for the individual church. I go to a web site and there is a tab that says ABOUT THE CHURCH. I figure, "Hey, here's where I can learn about the church, y'know, the folks that make up this menagerie of the Heaven bound." I hit the tab and I get info on the church building!

A Minister's Musing...in Shorts!

I don't want to know about the church building! The church building isn't going to Heaven. I can't just sit in it and catch a free ride. Peter tells me it's gonna get toasted along with everything else on Planet Here and never leave here. I wanna leave here and be in Heaven with Jesus and his church. I wanna be with the building up church here, not the built up church building.

Nuff said, however...

I want to spend my Sundays sitting around with other like-minded disciples of Christ and have my Bible open on my lap and a pen and paper at the ready and a cup of coffee next to me. I want to know what Jesus would have me to do come Monday morning when I have to end my weekend and get back out into the rat killing world and fight off Satan and keep myself unstained from the world. I want to be able to stop what I'm doing and pray for a brother or sister that has a big old heavy load on their life. [*"Goodness, is he wound up or what?!" "Just let it go, he's on a roll."*] I want to be able to sign a card for Sister Mabel who is having everything removed next Wednesday, and then put her on speakerphone as the church sings *Be With Me, Lord* and then prays for her well-being. I want to hear what Sister Suzy has to say about our Bible reading, and hear what Brother Furbie has to say instead of being locked into one person's half hour thoughts. If I sing a song, I want to read aloud the words and ask my brothers and sisters what that stanza means to them in this point in their lives instead of the lights going down and everyone reaching for the stars while fly encrusted children stand ankle deep in sludge up on the wall. I want to give of my hard earned money and have it go to those children and not the bug man next Friday as he sprays the edifice.

And, really, technology isn't all that it's cracked up to be. I got a voice message some time back from my buddy that I hang out with on a regular basis. We sit around and solve the world's problems, have a drink or so, talk about guns till we can't stand it anymore and then we go shoot those guns out in the desert. He simply called me to ask if Wednesday was a good time to hang out (yes, middle aged folks are allowed to hang). He doesn't have kids. Mine are grown and gone. None of them are named Troy. Neither he nor I have nicknames.

Now, his girlfriend might have given him a name like Snookie or BearBear, but I'm not privy to it and, besides, guys don't talk like that anyway because we would get beat up at the gym.

Anyway, my cellphone turns voice messages into text messages. How? I dunno. One of those things where one of my kids took the phone away from me, punched a few buttons, handed it back to me and said, "Here, try this out." Here's the message. I've saved it on my phone. I know how to do that.

Hey Pretty, it's Road Toast calling to see what you're up to. Joe Joe it's Troy! I was just calling to wake up to go bathroom and I was just calling to see if you can come on Wednesday. Anyway gimme a call if tomorrow's a good day for you and I was calling to let you know that your student Troy was absent from periods 12 and a while and looking at that 5:00 at the house time. Anyway gimme a call when you get this message and let me know. Talk to you later, bye.

Couldn't wait to show that one to him.

A lawyer stood up and put Jesus to the test, saying, "Teacher, what shall I do to inherit eternal life?" And Jesus answered, "What is written in the Law? How does it read to you?" Luke 10:25

Airports in the Circle of Life

And it came about when the Syrians had come into Samaria, that Elisha said, "O Lord, open the eyes of these soldiers." So the Lord opened their eyes, and the Syrians saw they were in the midst of their enemies, the Israelites. The king of Israel, when he saw this, said to Elisha, "My father, shall I kill them? Shall I kill them?"
II Kings 6

Caveat: If you have never been hospitalized for a complete psychotic break from reality or had to spend three weeks at "Happy Acres" because you don't remember the seventies, you will probably not understand fully the contents of this little happening some years ago.

Let's face it about airports. Where else on this raging planet can one spend all day, sit on wildly uncomfortable furniture, listen to a constant stream of unintelligible noises and voices coming over a half a million ceiling speakers, get run over by these rush carts full of sour faced people clutching their bags up under their chins, clutch your own bag up under your chin every time you go to the restroom, eat threefold overpriced food trying all the while to keep from making eye contact with anyone else and all of this for a small fortune that you had to pay out for the privilege just to hang out first at this end then the other--and all points in between!

If I were to get my Ph.D. in psychology, it would certainly be centered upon airport dynamics. You see, no one on the face of the earth lives their lives anything near what goes on inside an airport. No one's house is run this way. If your house is run this way, you are a sick puppy. There is help. Call 1-888-I-Am-Sick for a free brochure on how you and your family can begin to make steps to leading a normal life.

No one's office is run this way, either. Our country clubs do not resemble airports and neither do our places of entertainment. Not even do our Appalachian Snake Handling Revival Holiness Churches of the Apostolic Order come anywhere close to airport happenings. In short, airports are our lowest common denominator for Western Civilization. Let's start with the seven hundred and sixty-four magazine outlets in any given airport. For sure, *someone's* buying the magazines or else these gozillion shops couldn't stay in business. After all, we're not subsidizing these shops!

Are we?

Start by browsing through some of these magazines. You don't have to go past the cover. Take, for instance, the cover of *Cosmopolitan, GQ, Redbook, Seventeen* and even *People Mag.* Look carefully at those who grace the covers of those editions. Did you see anyone in the airport who remotely looked like anyone on the cover? Now one could cry foul, that this wasn't a sampling. You know, one of those random things that keeps coming up in tests. But it was, for you see some folks were from around there and some were not. That is the beauty of an airport--a random sampling of folks. Now go back and do it again, this time picking another magazine stand. Do not sample the same magazine stand twice--you make the sales clerk nervous and you will be tagged as 'one of those people.' It is in the airport that you can carry on a conversation with the magazine covers. Actually, the covers will start the conversation.

"Psst, hey buddy. You, too, can look like this."

"No I can't. I'm not genetically engineered or otherwise predisposed that way."

"Hey, just read my article on page twenty three and buy all of the products that I list and, yes, you will look like this. Just look at the cover at the beautiful people."

"But I'm in the over forty range, age wise. These people on the cover are my kids' age. I cannot look like that unless we can turn the clock back nearly thirty years."

"Oh, yes you can. This is tried and true. Works for millions."

"Where are they? I'm looking all over this airport. All I see is overweight, dumpy, pear shaped, saggy and a few folks that, when they walk, their behind looks like two raccoons fighting under a blanket." It is then that the other magazine covers begin to speak…

"Hey, sailor, does your wife look like me?"

Now at this point, I'm not going to go on about fightin' coons and such. I would probably get into trouble, but you get the drift. Bottom line (No pun intended here!)--and it can be proved in any airport on any day of the week--is that the stuff you see on the covers of magazines just doesn't happen in real life. So why do we spend so much time and money worrying about that which we couldn't genetically alter on a good day? Simple, we've been sold a bill of goods and the marketeers know it.

I'm all for beauty. Some wise man once said that beauty was only skin deep. However, ugly runs skin deep, too. Beauty is in the eyes of the beholder, we are told. Sad thing is that ugly is in the eyes of the beholder, also! But beauty shouldn't be limited to the latest styles and hairdos. Wrong clothes this season?--Ugly! See, that is all wrong. We should be a little more happy with the way things are.

Where does ugly come from and come in at? It comes from one's mouth and the life that they lead. Same place beauty comes from.

Yes, go ahead and spice it up a little. Let's not all go around looking like we just crawled out of the sack, but for Pete's sake, let's all get off of this eternal youth stuff. I don't know about you, but I wouldn't go back to being twenty five years younger if you paid me. Actually, you would have to pay me--and pay me big time--to go back that many years because I remember being flat broke then, driving something that just barely hung together and working a job that busted my hump and made me extra tired at the end of the day. I also worried myself to death about the next zit eruption back then. Nope, I'm off the Craters of the Moon scene. I like being forty...or so.

So my philosophy about airports is this, and it is a twofold advice to both men and women. First, the fairer sex:

Girls! Get off of it and relax a bit. Doesn't matter if you are eighteen, thirty eight or fifty eight. Doesn't matter if you are five pounds overweight or thirty five--you don't need to kill yourself. Doesn't matter if you have the latest poodle-doo out of the pages of Primp or you are paler than a bed sheet. It doesn't matter if you look forty, if you are forty. You earned it! A bulge or a spot or a stretch mark doesn't disqualify you as Miss America. After all, you only have to hold that title for one. And rest assured that you do. Read Proverbs 31. King Lemuel hit the nail on the head.

Now for the men. Do not stand around the magazine shop at the airport, thumbing through all the magazines for hours on end. It makes the magazine shop clerks nervous.

I finalized these thoughts about the airports and the circle of life on an earlier trip, returning from Dallas-Ft. Worth airport to Portland, Oregon via Phoenix and Boston. I know, I know. It was the milk run, but the tickets were reasonable. I received all the time I needed for this finalization. I hadn't planned on it--the extra time that is. The little trolls that work secretly underground in each airport planned it.

You think I'm kidding. You didn't read the Time article, I suppose. Each airport (FAA ruling, 1976) is equipped with an underground room which is staffed with highly trained, FAA regulated trolls. Not for Flight Control. No that is done way upstairs in those pointy, all glass towers. No, this is for Control of Flights. You know, those hundreds of monitors that lace the hallways of airports that keep catching the attention of any and everybody that walks to and fro. In fact, not many can pass a single bank of monitors without looking. The FAA knows this and trains their trolls accordingly.

Now remember, a Troll is a Troll and is not to be confused with a Gnome. I realize that they tend to look quite a bit alike, but let's get real here. There are such things as Gnomes and most Gnomes are employed in large metropolitan areas to do such things as mess with traffic and walk/don't walk signals. Occasionally they will put little signs out that say such things as 'Construction Ahead' or 'Detour' when there really isn't anything going on construction wise. This is why I don't choose to live in an overly huge metropolitan area--Metro Gnomes!

By now, if this is your first introduction to the idea, you have guessed that the job of the Airport Troll is to keep you stressed out and nervous. We expect it. We actually love it! For days before we have to leave on a trip, we begin to bemoan the fact that we 'hafta go to the airport.' All of our listeners will begin to bite their lip, shake their head and relate stories of the last time they had to go to the airport--even if it was just to pick someone up (It is, in fact, the same phenomena as recounting surgeries--"I almost *died* from that surgery!"). The government knows this tendency towards nervousness and has poured millions of tax dollars (if not billions) into creating the atmosphere. This is why your tickets are so high.

But why trolls? Because that's just the way that it is. Trolls--and I don't want to sound racist here or otherwise non-PC--are best suited for the job. For as far back as anyone can remember, trolls handle this kind of work.

So there I am at the counter of America West Airlines, or AWA (AWA is, interestingly enough when voiced, the sound that a baby makes. Many adults make that sound, too, when their flight is canceled, baggage lost, *etc.*). I have forty minutes to make the gate. Fair enough, I believe, and the counter person tells me the same.

"Where are you going?" I'm asked.

Now wouldn't it be better if they would find out who I was first and not where I'm going? She did finally ask me if I had a name, but this particular order smacks more of loading cows or sheep into one of those huge trucks that makes us nervous on the highway and smells bad. For barnyard animals on their way to slaughter, destination is far more of a concern than individual animal names.

"Do you have luggage today, Mr. Pennington?"

I assume that the Mr. is to make up for the cattle call I received earlier in our conversation. Yes, of course I have bags. Everyone has bags. No one gets on a plane without luggage of some kind. We are all going *somewhere* for a period of time. We are *flying* because we do-not-have-time-to-drive. We require a change of underwear in case we are in an accident, toothpaste, deodorant, combs if you have hair. Just once I'd like to say that I don't have bags. I decide that today is that day!

"I don't have any bags today. Maybe tomorrow."

"What is that in your hand then, Mr. Pennington?"

"A growth. Doctors give me six months."

Now the next line of questioning is serious. I'm all for airport security. If I'm going to Philadelphia to see great aunt Mabel, I don't want to sit on a runway in South America while some drug crazed lunatic bargains me for money. But just once...

"Did you pack these bags yourself, Mr. Pennington?"

"No, I'm only forty something right now. Don't push me. My mother packed them for me so that I don't wrinkle my underwear. It's the hospital thing, you know."

"Have these bags been with you for the entire time you have been in the airport?"

"No, I first noticed these bags staring at me. Then they left the bar and began to follow me. I felt so uncomfortable. Now they sort of talked themselves into my life. I'm such a weak willed person!" At this point, you should break down into tears and tell how you have been going to a therapist for several years and even joined a group on Monday nights, sacrificing football, so that you can become a stronger person and learn to say, "No!" and mean it.

But once again I weenied out and simply answered her questions like she was my third grade teacher. When the ticket counter lady cleared me and my bags, I entered the secure zone. Entering in the secure zone makes us nervous--and this was well before 9/11. Not being in the zone itself, but the act of actually getting in there. You know the feeling. People file through the magnetic resonance sucker that looks all the world like a medieval wedding trellis, with keys, loose change and watches already removed from the person to expedite matters. Suddenly, the alarm goes off on a kindly looking business man or some lady who could be anyone's grandmother in small town USA. With the simple beep of the alarm, panic begins to race and rage through those not yet cleared. The questions begin to race through our minds also: "Did I get everything? What are my socks made of? Will I have to endure a strip search here in public? Do I have a steel plate in my head and no one told me?" The kid in me has always wanted to dive head first onto the conveyer belt, then ask if they saw any malignant tumors as I come out the other side.

Before I took my seat by the gate, I had to walk past the monitors. Knowing what I know--and you now know--

A Minister's Musing...in Shorts!

about the monitors, I refused to look at first. After sitting by the boarding gate counter for an eternity of five minutes, it became more than I could bear. Add to that the fact that others were lining up to all ask questions of the people behind the gate counter. My nervousness increased. I had to examine the monitors.

Trying to look as calm and collected as I could, I approached the monitors. It is then that I realized I had doofed. Doofed is when you find yourself staring at the incoming flights when you need outgoing, or vice versa. I shifted 4 paces left, hoping that no one, especially females, saw me doof. This technique is called the Lateral UnDoofing. We probably don't do it often enough.

Then I panicked. My flight wasn't on there. It was one of those moments when you have to take a triple take, moving your eyes from ticket to monitor and repeat, repeat. It wasn't there. Sure, I had the AWA monitors and knew right away that the trolls had returned from brunch. Like the front lines of a battlefield for a side who is being beaten back, the gate counter had long been abandoned. Back to the ticket counter, this time as a statistic.

"What happened to my flight from DFW to Phoenix?"

"It was canceled."

"What about the leg from Phoenix to Boston to home?"

It is at this time that the ticket lady's face turns to deadpan and she begins to furiously type on the keyboard. She typed and she typed, all the while staring at the screen. One day I will check out the phenomena, but I have noticed that at many ticket counters the keyboard simply isn't plugged into anything. Perhaps a stall tactic.

"That flight is on time!" she said it with a gleeful smile and a bit of a singsongy wave that young girls do when they talk about a boyfriend. The kind of smile that someone gives you when they are new on a job and they haven't dealt with their hundredth customer and been chewed out royally by the management.

"How will I get on that flight if this one is canceled?"

"I'll have to get my supervisor on that one. Just a minute."

The supervisor emerged. Lady in her mid-fifties. Starched uniform. Massive chest muscles with a name tag that read

'Olga.' Forearms and legs to match, with her red hair done up in the double ram's horns buns. Yardstick in one hand and a pencil through one of the buns. It WAS my third grade teacher. I couldn't figure out what I had done, but I knew I was either going to have to write something a hundred times or be transported to a fifteenth century dungeon. I was wrong. I had forgotten one of the basic rules of the airport. The Troll is the enemy, not the ticket people.

However, counter people in airports are funny as a general rule. Maybe not the enemy, but you can learn a lot about human nature by studying counter people. The Phoenix airport finally did rise out of the ashes and into my reality. Now shaken, and not wanting to leave the gate area for anything, I was mainly left with nothing to do. I had begun to wonder about the mystery of the white paging phones. There was, I noticed, a steady stream of folks--plain folks like you and me--being constantly called to the white paging phones for a message. I had six such phones in my line of sight but never once saw anyone advance and step up to the challenge of answering one. Maybe some evil lurked here that I was heretofore unfamiliar with. I decided that this was a bit much for me to digest on this trip, so I rearranged this opportunity of time to watch instead the gate version of the ticket counter people.

I've already alluded to the fact that people get jumpy at gate counters. The gate counter can be clear as the desert sky, then some passenger will look intently at his ticket, muse and humph a little, then cock his head to one side. After a moment of careful thought, he will position his bags under his chair and head for the counter. Folks will strain to listen in on the conversation, but the Orwellian droning of the various and sundry loudspeakers calling plain folks to the white paging phones will prevent reception. Then the situation is heightened when the counter person begins to clack relentlessly on the unplugged keyboard while the passenger stands nervously by, shifting from first one foot to the other. The result? Chain reaction.

I tend to label this situation as cold fusion. Fusion speaks of the melding and combining of people in a rapid state at the counter. Cold is the type of sweat. The cowboys on the

Goodnight-Loving Trail would have used the term stampede. While in Phoenix, I couldn't help myself.

Forty five minutes is a long time to wait if you have already scoped the people and magazine covers out, and read every newspaper that has been left in the seating area. Everyone was calm, and even a few were dozing.

Two counter people had mounted their position, but had drawn no nervous glances. Like the little boy who can't help but unmercifully drag the stick up and down the fence while the dog barks on the other side, I sprang into action.

I suddenly bolted in my seat and stiffened my legs. I kept my eyes wide open and grabbed my ticket out of my bag. I gave it a stare, then shook my head and grabbed my glasses to throw them on. In a full twisting dismount from my seat, I rose and simultaneously kicked my bag under it and headed straight for the ticket counter. Keeping my voice low so as to build suspense in the already alerted passengers, I handed the ticket to Counter Person A and asked if 14D were an aisle, window or squeeze. Now for all anyone else knew, I was asking if this were indeed the correct flight to Portland and if we were going to stop off in Anchorage or Khartum along the way. Of course, with any question--even as simple as the seating assignment--there must come at least 30 seconds of intense pounding on the keyboard. She must have thought I had lost my mind when, upon hearing 'aisle,' that I shook my head and loudly said, "Oh, dear." I had other intentions.

When I left the counter, I was already enveloped in a sea of people. Panic People. All with tickets waving and wild eyes. Sweat was beginning to show through many folk's shirt backs and underarms as the line began to snake around the pillars. I picked up my bag and repositioned myself for a side shot to the side show. You never heard two girls do more clacking on unplugged keyboards in your life.

Finally, the last customer was satiated and sat down. Fifteen minutes to go and nothing for me to do. It is then that one of the clackers produced the biggest Butterfinger candy bar out of her purse that you have ever seen. It was the Dollar Giant, but since she was barely five foot and under 110, it seemed like a rolled up Sunday Times, only chocolate covered. She said something to the other disheveled keyboard clacker, then in one orchestrated move, took a huge bite of it as she squatted down behind the counter, thus becoming invisible. Unless one had positioned himself correctly.

I moved once again to the counter and approached the standing one.

"Thank you for flying with AWA today! How may I help you?" It almost had a melody. It was also to my advantage that they had forgotten the stampede I started just a half hour ago.

"I would like to speak to the other counter person, please."

"There's no one here but me, sir."

"What about the one (and I bent my index finger so as to point up and over) down there?"

"She's on a break, sir. How may I help you today?"

"But I have an important message from higher up to give to her. It is very important."

With that, the squatting clacker stood straight up, cheeks bulging. I've read the ingredients on a Butterfinger. Simple. Corn Flakes, peanut butter and lots and lots of crunchy type sugar and a little partially hydrolyzed animal fat and/or partially hydrogenated palm kernel oil masquerading as chocolate. Some was sprinkled in and around her lips. Some was shelved on her vest. Vast amounts were in the process of being predigested through mastication. I continued.

"How are you today?"

"*Mphrim Nawlrod.*" She blew some Butterfinger on the counter and on her keyboard.

"Oh, I'm sorry. Got the wrong person. Please resquat and continue hydrolyzed animal fat mastication."

Though I must admit that AWA did a great job of delivering my luggage to my door the next day by noon, it is still a hassle to get somewhere and the rest of you simply isn't there waiting on you on those carousel thingies. Somehow, to pre-proclaim the term 'lost' on luggage is spooky. One wonders if one doesn't somehow magically mojo luggage into oblivion by using those terms. I knew I had to go to baggage claim and do the dance. I vowed not to use the term *lost*.

"I made it, but my baggage didn't. What do I need to do now?"

"Did you check your luggage with *us*?"

Now if she means by us the people in that particular room, then no I didn't. I did that with some similarly dressed people, but that was hundreds of miles away. During the wagon train days, we would have measured the distance in months. Now if she meant by us the AWA as a corporation, then she is right on target. But, then again, that would be a somewhat slap in the face to think that she thinks that I'm dumb enough to go check my bags with Continental or TWA or Southwest or Greyhound or Checker Cab Co. and then go get on a different colored airplane...

What has all of this got to do with the Circle of Life? Well, to begin with, the title was catchy, I thought.

But let's be real here. You aren't going to win in an airport. You will be stressed out by all of the people you are crunched in with. You will go on the brink of insanity with the omnipresent noises and squawks over the speakers calling who knows who to the white paging phones. You will be nervous to the point of breaking out in hives. You will never see anyone on a white paging phone. You will be broke when you walk out, and you will walk out alone, all of your dirty underwear being somewhere in another airport.

If I were you, I would take the bus.

Bus Twilight Zones

This is pure and undefiled religion in the sight of our God and Father, to visit orphans and widows in their distress, and to keep oneself unstained by the world. **James 1:27**

Kindness cannot correct the past. Kindness can, however, make the here and now right.

When I was younger, Rod Serling used to entertain us every week by taking us to a place that was beyond imagination. Perhaps not beyond our imagination but at least beyond what we would have imagined if we slowed down long enough to imagine something. Many of the episodes had one thing in common--the feeling of being stuck either in a place or a situation that seemed predictable until the final outcome came along and changed everything: a man with broken glasses stuck on the steps of a library; an astronaut stuck on a planet; a man stuck in a spaceship with a cook book; a woman stuck in her car for fear of seeing the hitchhiker again; a woman stuck in her cabin with tiny spacemen. And so they went, week after week, thrilling us with yet another outcome after many turns and twists.

In everyday life, it is hard to duplicate the Twilight Zone, for often our lives are so predictable that they become boring. We punctuate our lives with vacations and trips that are themselves almost as predictable, thereby never creating that sense of relief brought about only by the little twists and turns of unpredictability. I have, in the recent past, discovered a place where Rod Serling would not look out of place if he were to step on to the scene. That place is the bus terminal. The what?! Yes, the bus terminal. The Greyhound Central of any city, anywhere. Purely by accident I decided some while ago to take the bus instead of either driving or flying. It's not that I can't drive--I drive quite well. It's not that I have a fear of flying--I don't. I do have a fear of crashing, but everyone has that. I don't, however, object to hurling 350 mph, seven miles above the ground. Piece of cake. I do, however, object to being stripped, searched and have my luggage mangled. It's not that I can't afford anything but the bus. No, I am rich compared to most folks on this planet.

It's not that I have a bus fetish--I don't, and don't know anyone who does. OK, I did see some derelicts hanging out in the Denver bus station that may have had a fetish, but most folks don't. I just wanted to do something different, so I did. Whenever possible, I will take the bus from now on. Busses have something that appeals to me--scores of people trying to get from point A to point B, trying to get by on as little funds as possible. Is there a distinct *kind* of person that usually rides the bus lines instead of fly? Well, you know that answer. Busses aren't for the well-to-do. But listen to Rod:

Meet John Doe. A little man trying to get from one town to the next, believing he can make this happen at the bus terminal. He enters the station, bags in hand, believing he will accomplish this task, but before the night is over he will be changed by experiences that can only be found in...The Bus Twilight Zone.

People are either sheep or cattle. Both animals have a strong herd instinct, as we do. If we believe a line is forming, we will queue up often not knowing who called the line or even where the line is going to end. This is only intensified when we are away from home and the object of the moment is to get home. Pushing through the checkout line so we can go home has spawned Supermarket Rage. We all know Airport Rage. Road Rage isn't even news anymore. Bus Terminal Rage gets no mention in the pop psychology books or the evening news. It should.

Two o'clock in the morning is a time for sleeping unless one has a night job or is forced to stand guard duty somewhere. Our circadian rhythm demands that we are not our best at 2 a.m., regardless of the amount of coffee or naps we have had. It is a time when an otherwise selfless person will indeed become very selfish and fold into Mr. Me mode rather quickly. However, Mr. Me mode has its limitations when an unwritten line gets crossed. I turn your attention to a bus terminal in Amarillo, Texas at about 2 a.m. on a pretty warm summer night.

Lines to go west began to form. No one behind the counter called for a line, it is just the lines that seem to form out of fear, anxiety, unsurety and the Mr. Me factor. One line began to form inside the terminal at door number three and another line began to form outside door number three on the patio. Each line thought theirs was the correct line.

"I don't know why those people are lining up outside on the patio, they won't load us except from in here. I ride through here all the time and we always load from the inside."

"I don't know why those people think they can load inside the terminal. The bus parks out here. Do they think that Greyhound is gonna carry them out here and put them on the bus?"

One of the outside liner uppers was a black gentleman and his very elderly mother. You may, at this point, question why I would call this man black. Because he was--and still is, I presume. People are what they are and sometimes it figures into a story. One of the inside liner uppers was a very hyperactive white man who was very vociferous about those who were lining up outside. By and by the innies won and the outies were called back into the terminal via the loud speaker as the bus began to roll into the station. That's when the line got crossed.

It would have been enough to just have the outies walk silently past the innies and move to the back of the line. That would have been President Lincoln's approach had he still been around. He wanted the beaten South to simply get back in line with no further punishment. He would have called all the outies in and told the innies to keep their mouths shut. That was all that the innies were going to do. After all, it was after two in the morning and we all had a bus to catch. Nervous white guy, however, couldn't let it go. He began to rail on the beaten South as they walked by and laid down their weapons at our feet.

"Ha! Ha ha--HA! I t-o-l-d, TOLD you bunch that you needed to be in here!" Quiet little *"whatever's"* began to pour forth from both sides, trying to shut the man up. It didn't do

A Minister's Musing...in Shorts!

any good, the white man stepped it up a bit: as he kicked a bag on the floor, he exclaimed, "If you *niggers* wouldn't stand outside we could already be gone by now."

It wasn't so much the *N*-word as it was the bag sliding across the floor and knocking the elderly mother down from her wanted position of holding her son's arm to steady herself, into a position of being flat on her back on the bus station floor. Some people in this country don't have an N word line, however, everyone in this country has a line when old ladies get knocked down to the floor because of Mr. Me.

I happened to be standing behind nervous white guy, or now, Mr. Me. After several years of quelching fights and such between prisoners, I instinctively grabbed his arms in a pin-type fashion. A big hulking white man whose hands were so big that to shake hands with him would be like putting your hand in a catcher's mitt, took the opportunity to break Mr. Me's nose and a rib with two quick punches that only the camera could catch. That's when bus driver moved into the scene.

Now, picture bus driver who now had all eyes on him for several reasons. Reason number one was that he was the driver, a sort of authority figure that everyone looked to at the moment. Reason two, the driver was black and after all, the N word had been used. Reason three, if you thought Punching Man was big, Driver looked as if he could hold the bus up with one arm and change the tire with the other and never sweat.

"Did you see that?!? Did-you-see-that?!? That man hit me," said the whiny little white guy who was trying desperately to regain his supposed dignity--and stop his nose from gushing blood.

"Mister," said the very big, very black bus driver, "The only thing I see right now is a little old lady being picked up off the floor."

A moment of silence, then the moment of truth. Mr. Me's lips began to try to form letters, then finally, "Are you going to let me on the bus?"

"You bet," Driver began, "but you best not fall asleep after I turn off the lights. It gets real dark on that bus and I can't see a dang thing going on sometimes (he waived his hands around with his eyes squinted shut as if blind). I'd suggest that you sit *real close* to all of your *friends* on this five hour ride."

A Healthy Thing Should Look Like This!

So-called reality TV has taken hold of our psyche. Amid chants of voting him off the bus, we pulled away--leaving one very white, very 'me' oriented man clutching his bags sitting on a bench. He was experiencing the Twilight Zone of his own doing. At the first break where we all got off the bus to hit the snack bar, the big slugging white guy thanked me profusely for 'setting him up a shot.' He broke into a big smile that proudly showed off all five of his teeth.

I realized, maybe for the first time, that kindness cannot correct the past. Kindness can, however, make the here and now right.

Because I was secretly on the lookout for another episode on my next bus ride, I picked a seat that was in the far corner of the now vacated, very old and decaying, Fort Worth bus terminal. From that vantage point, I was able to see everything that was going on, everyone who was coming or going. That's when I was approached by the white, armed security guard. Because of experience, I could tell by the way he walked--and the way he had his duty belt arranged--that this man was a retired police officer. He walked right up into my personal space as I sat there in the corner minding my own business.

"What would you say if I asked you to move so I could sit in that seat?" he more demanded than asked.

"I would say, 'No.'"

"I've got a PR-24 right here that says you need to move," as he put his hand on his night stick baton, "What do you think of that?"

"I've got a brand new pair of tennis shoes that I can connect right up to your crotch or knee caps before you could draw that baton. What do you think of that?"

Well, he laughed. I laughed. He said he hadn't had that much fun all week. Truth be told, he wanted to sit there because that particular chair was out of camera range. I told him that working Corrections for years gave me a pretty good understanding of what he was asking. I slid down to the end of the short bench, putting an empty space between the two of us.

"Yep, you see it all in a bus station," he began our conversation together, "It's like a while ago, there was a knucklehead in the bathroom all spread out and bathing in three sinks...Hey," and pointed to a middle aged black man across the aisle. "You're the knucklehead. Get over here!" And the man moved to the seat in-between two ex-cops--and into our little party--as the security officer got out his night stick and tapped the bathroom bathing black man on the knees.

"I'm gonna break your kneecaps with this thing if you didn't clean up the sink back there. Tell me you cleaned it up so I don't hafta break your legs."

"Well, I've been listening to you two. I don't think you'll hit me or I'll sic this big white guy sitting next to me onto you and he'll kick you with his new tennies. I'd think you would rather keep what he said he was gonna kick on you."

Maybe you had to be there. Maybe it was the time of night, but we were all three laughing and carrying on like little boys. Nothing on earth besides the Twilight Bus Zone could have put the three of us together. A chance triangulation on the street could not have produced the laughter. The bus ticket may have cost $118, but the moment was priceless.

We talked about bus rides, jail, places to eat in Cleveland, arresting knuckleheads at two a.m., weather, holidays, stress and stuffed animals. As we hit the stress subject cross bred with long layovers, the man in the middle said he saw a lot of stressed out people over the last several days on his long bus journey across America. He even remarked that a black woman in her late thirties or early forties across the aisle looked stressed. That's when he said loudly to her, "Sister, are you all right?"

"I thinks so." Her eyes immediately began to dart back and forth across the bus station as she tightened her grip on her belongings already sitting tightly in her lap. "I'm going backs to Mississippi to see if I gots a home, you know, Hurricane Katrina and all that stuff. They said I hads to go home now and put me on the bus."

At that moment I began to fade from the conversation. A gift (or curse) of perception began to tell me that everything wasn't all right with the woman who sat clutching a few plastic shopping bags so close you might have thought they were gold bars. Her clothing said it wasn't gold and her eyes continuously darted from one information board to another, while she clutched and rubbed a ticket in her hand. I told my good tyme buddies, "scuse me."

"Ma'am, where did you say you were going?" as I took a seat next to her. I knew my new found friends would watch my baggage.

"I'm going backs to Mississippi to see if I gots a home. They put me on the bus and says it was time to go backs to Mississippi but I don't know if I gots a home but I will go backs to see."

"Did you get here just tonight?"

"Oh, no. They put me on the bus a few days ago and I'm supposed to go backs to my home if I gots one. You know, Hurricane Katrina and all that stuff."

"May I look and see your ticket? You can hold it and just show me what bus you are supposed to get on." She held her ticket so I could see it, but held it so tight that I would have ripped it had I tried to take it. The grip on the ticket said she didn't trust me, her eyes were crying out 'for God's sake, somebody help me!' Her bus had pulled out earlier that day. She had missed it because it didn't have MISSISSIPPI on the lighted sign on the front. In a closer review of her ticket, I could tell that missing her bus had been more of the norm over the past few days and not the exception.

"May I speak to a supervisor?" as I approached the desk. My inquiry into her situation was met with a rather coldish, "People miss the bus all the time and just have to take the next one…" The next one would be leaving in 45 minutes and would have HOUSTON on the light board.

"Ma'am, your bus homeward will be here in 45 minutes. Can you see that clock over there? Your bus will have HOUSTON on the front and will be here at 7:55. That's the one you want."

Some people are slow. It's inevitable. They define the fast ones. But no one should be allowed to rot in a bus station because they are slow. While I'm talking with the lady and wishing like all hell that my bus wasn't going to leave before hers, a forty-ish nondescript white guy came over and squatted down in front of the lady.

"I believe you and I are going the same direction. See, here's my ticket to Mississippi and I'm gonna be on the same bus as you are. You can sit next to me if you want to so you don't get lost." DON'T GET LOST. Those words had a ring to them that went in somewhere deep inside everything she was.

For me, I've never been lost. Not that kind of lost. I got lost backpacking in the Big Bend desert once, but had it straightened up within two days. No, I'm talking about the lost look when a family comes home to a burned down house. The lost look that a widow has who has long shut herself up in a dark house after the death of her direction. The look across someone's face after a complete mental collapse and break from reality. The lost look across the face of the POW, who wonders what went terribly wrong. This woman was lost in a sea of people, but to look deep into her pupils revealed a tiny thread of a return to normal, a hope of the long fearful ordeal being over.

I sat back down, but not for long. The rather coldish lady was barking "Amarillo" and I gathered my stuff to get into the lineup. A quick glance at the security guard caught him giving me the universal 'I'm-going-to-keep-my-eye-on-her' look. I saw a little black girl of about five come up and give the lost lady a cold soda from the vending machine, simply holding it out--wordless--for her to take, take away some of the pain of rotting in bus terminal after bus terminal.

Standing in line I heard a new, yet familiar voice talking to me. It was my sink bathing friend whom I had earlier saved his kneecaps from a most dreadful ordeal. He held out a hand and asked if he could shake mine. Not perhaps understanding the moment, I held out my hand. All the years in the oil drilling business, law enforcement and pastoring, I bet I shook about 5,000 hands a year. This was not one of those 'howarya' shakes. It was a firm but gentle grasp. His only words were, "Hey, you did right by that sister."

As I boarded the bus, I began to look for empty seats, the bus being a third full having come from Dallas. Having reverted to 'me' mode, I missed the elderly man sitting with his arms folded tightly across his middle. He was shivering from the cold night air coming into the bus along with the passengers. This elderly black man sat with his stocking cap on looking blankly out of the window, hoping to get the bus doors closed and get moving again soon.

A Healthy Thing Should Look Like This!

A young Hispanic fellow, decked out in gangland baggies and hip-hop shades dropped under his chin stopped dead in the aisle and asked, "Hey, *viejo*, are you cold?" The old man just looked at him and shook his head in the affirmative. The boy took his coat off and placed it around the old man and said, "Shoot, dawg, I'll sit here. I'm so fat that I'll keep both us warm. Where are you going? I'm going to Atlanta..." I sat down and looked across the aisle at the scene. A Jewish carpenter told a story once of a Samaritan businessman who stopped to help a pretty banged-up Jew. He didn't need to. The two races didn't get along. No one would have even thought of holding the Samaritan accountable for anything had he chosen to keep going. No, but he wanted to help and his story will forever be preserved as the way things *ought* to be.

That same Carpenter could have just as easily told the story of the fat Latino and the shivering old black man. The boy didn't know it, nor was he aware of Heaven itself bestowing the right of that boy at that very moment to call himself a man for the rest of his life. I lay the seat back and was asleep before we were out of downtown Fort Worth.

I realized, maybe for the first time, that kindness doesn't correct the past. It simply makes the here and now right.

Same route: Albuquerque to Fort Worth. Same time: night. Layover: once again, in Amarillo. Young mother, perhaps only just into her mid-twenties, struggling with a herd of bags and two girls, three and three months. It was evident by her luggage that she was headed somewhere for a very long time.

I've had little kids. I've traveled with them. It isn't easy, even when things are going very well. For this mother, it wasn't. The baby was becoming fussy and the little three year old was waking up. I sat next to their little carved out corner, knowing there was a story that was to unfold.

"It's hard traveling with small children, isn't it?" I opened the door of conversation.

"Yes, we have a long way to go. Just left Albuquerque. What about you?"

We talked of Albuquerque--what we liked and didn't. I explained I worked with children for a living, trying to keep her at ease talking to a strange, funny walking man more than twice her age. I offered the three year old some stick gum and she took two. I held the baby while Mom went to the restroom. She watched my bags and I made the same trip. I found rather quickly that they were 'going my way' but much further. Soon, it was time to board east. Mom had more luggage than she had hands.

"Let me help you with your stuff."

"Oh, no, I can get it." She tried, but she was simply reenacting her boarding in Albuquerque. Perhaps she had someone there to start her on her journey. Perhaps she was trying to maintain composure and not impose on a cripple. She loaded up kids and a few bags hanging on her shoulders. I gathered up the rest and boarded the bus ahead of her, finding her a seat opposite of mine.

"Thank you, sir," as she put her two children into seats for the next five or so hours. Soon, all three were fast asleep. At four in the morning, all children should be asleep. So should their parents.

Quick stop in Wichita Falls. If one didn't eat in Amarillo, then this was it. Bus stops for fifteen minutes--and the bus driver will leave you if not back on the bus. I was hungry, no starved! I didn't want to get off the bus in Fort Worth and have my family change their schedule to feed a starving man. As we pulled into the stop, the three year old woke up.

"I'm hungry, Mama."

"I know you are. We'll get something to eat when we get to Houston."

"How long is that?!" and there was distress in the little girl's voice.

I don't know what their story was. Was Mom running from someone or something? I didn't know. Was she lacking in the provision department for her two children, or was she simply on the bus out of distress and end-of-the-rope? It doesn't matter. What mattered was that there was a child, and she was hungry. Houston was an easy ten or twelve more hours away. I could tell by the little girl's response to her mother's now lost explanation that this wasn't the first time the little girl had heard the pronouncement of no food on the near horizon. I pulled out a twenty.

"Please, take this and get your kids and yourself something to eat."

"Oh, we don't have any money. I can't pay you back."

I can't pay you back... I wonder how many times the Jewish carpenter has heard the same line from people...and wondered himself. "Naw, take it. This was free. The money fairy dropped this in my wallet back in Amarillo. I'll watch your kids. Better hurry."

Soon, milk and other bus-manageable foods appeared. The three year old wasted no time. Mom wasted no time, either. It was only after we pulled away that she remembered the change.

"Nope, don't need it back. Remember, that was free money from the money fairy."

She knew I was lying to her. She had learned long ago when her childhood ended that there were no fairies and no free money. "But you didn't get anything to eat. Do you want some of this?"

"Nope, I'm not hungry, just sleepy." I turned my head to the window, hoping that my stomach wouldn't growl loud enough for her to hear. As the bus pulled into Fort Worth hours later, I reached into my bag for the only thing I had to eat--a small, bite sized candy bar. I wanted desperately to unwrap it and choke it down, but decided to offer it to the three year old. Houston was still maybe six hours away.

I realized, maybe for the first time, that kindness doesn't correct the past. It simply makes the here and now right.

Little children, let us not love with word or with tongue, but in deed and truth. I John 3:18

The Gate Keepers

Woe to you Pharisees! For you are like concealed tombs, and the people who walk over them are unaware of it.

One of the lawyers said to Jesus in reply, "Teacher, when You say this, You insult us too."

There have been many reasons put forth for the actions and attitudes of the Pharisees of the first century. Some say that they were devout. Jesus would disagree with that. Others would say that they were doing the best they could with what they had. Jesus would disagree with that. What they had was the exact equivalent of what we call today the Old Testament. The same lessons and conclusions we are allowed to draw today from it could have been drawn from it then. What we had with the Pharisees, plain and simple, were rule makers.

When a person or a group of persons decides that they have the will and wishes of God down clearly, a stake is driven in the ground. Never mind that the will and wishes of God just might extend far beyond that stake of personal understanding, the stake is driven nonetheless. More often than not, the stake is a ruling on a social custom or practice of the time. More often than not, folks get hurt by the ruling.

After a few stakes are driven into the land we call the grace of God, a pattern begins to emerge. That pattern is dissected, discussed, analyzed, critiqued and reviewed until someone decides that this stake is clearly a point that no one should go past, a line in the sand that shouldn't be crossed. Inside the stakes are safe areas and outside the staked area suddenly becomes a vast gray area of unknown territory. Then, like a repeat of history, a wire is strung between the stakes.

A fence is born.

Like the sailors and explorers of old who used to hug the coastlines of Europe, Africa and Asia--for fear of falling off the end of the earth--the fence brings a false sense of comfort and security. Even the fence line is something that becomes unapproachable, off limits.

However, a fence without a break is a useless fence, if one wishes to be inside of it and coax others into it. But to those outside the fence, a break in the fence is neither helpful nor of any consequence. Since we have an overwhelming urge to name things, we call those breaks gates. Gates work both ways, both to let in and to let out.

Since the fence is made of rules, the gate requires a gatekeeper. It must, for someone must be responsible for allowing both ingress and egress across fence lines--and what those lines represent. The position of Gatekeeper is not a position that any rational human being would either want or would it be a position to be sought after. Unless something is wrong with their thinking.

And so were the Pharisees. A rational person would see the Pharisees for what they were: men who would tie little scrolls of Scripture to their hair and beards (and sewed into the lining of their New Testament robes) while they meticulously separated even the smallest little items such as spices into equal parts of ten so they could give one of those portions into the Temple spice box! Their rules required flow charts that would rival any corporation's board meetings. Each time something new in society came forth, the flow chart would need to be extended and the fence would need to be adjusted, resulting in yet another human being suddenly finding himself on the outside of the safe zone and the gate shut.

For the time being, let's put the Pharisees aside. Don't put them up, for we will need to dust them off and bring them out again in a little while. In their place, let's focus for a while on a day in the life of Jesus, while He traveled with His apostles.

Mark chapter nine holds a short little story of the Apostle John announcing victoriously to Jesus that he had attempted to chase off someone who was casting out demons. To be sure, the unknown to us man was casting them out by the authority of Jesus, but wasn't actually part of the little band of twelve that were following Jesus day after day. Jesus corrects John with a stinging lesson even for today: just because that particular person wasn't traveling with Jesus and the twelve, it doesn't mean that they aren't sanctioned! Jesus rebuked John before the first strand of wire could be strung. The lesson is learned, but we are not given any more information as to the identity of the man who was casting out demons.

This story introduces you to that man. In reality this story shows us all men who would stand inside of the grace of God, but standing outside of the fence.

A man came into the Sunday morning Bible class with one thing on his mind: his mother. To be sure, she had not taken care of herself during her fifty-seven years on earth. She had lived it up in the late sixties and early seventies, but that ultimately gave way to simply alcohol and cigarettes, and way too much reliance on over-the-counter remedies of all flavors. However, she was ill. Her son explained that her zyme n' lyte panels didn't look all that good, though he neither knew what that meant nor could he produce a number. There was talk of autobodies and syndromes, operations and recoveries, although the young man didn't know what it all meant--and many in the Bible class pretended to by nodding their heads.

All he knew was that his mother was sick and the overall outlook didn't look so well.

He had one request and that was for a prayer of healing for his mother. He knew that he, along with his wife and children, hadn't been to church anywhere on a regular basis, but knew that there was a God in Heaven that both cared and could heal. However, his timing wasn't the best in the world, since he had pretty much blurted out the whole ordeal about his mother during the teacher's lesson, although he believed it was relevant since the class was discussing the bronze serpent in Numbers. Seeing he had the floor, he pulled out a 5x7 picture of his mother and handed it to the teacher.

"If you could please stand my mother's picture up against the teaching stand so everyone can see her…please?" The man had eyes full of both tears and anticipation for what God would shortly do on his mother's behalf. "Thank you, and

A Healthy Thing Should Look Like This!

could you hang this little silver cross over the picture, also? Now my request is that if there is a man or woman here that is one of God's designated prayer warriors, I know that God will hear you since you have the gift of intercession. Who is the designated prayer warrior in this group?" Suddenly, the anticipation in his eyes began to turn to one of shame and embarrassment as the room hushed--as if on cue. The class leader broke the icy silence.

"Is your mother a Christian?" --- "Well, yes, she is." --- "Is she a member of the church?" --- "Well, yes, she is." --- Which congregation is she a member of?" --- "I think she goes to the Believers Fellowship Center." --- "Oh, I see..." and the teacher's voice and eyes began to trail off into the two dozen people assembled in the classroom. The classroom's occupants began to stiffen even more, as if on cue.

The wrong flavor of church had been mentioned. It wasn't the same as theirs. Eyes continued to look downward. A noticeable strain came across the teacher's face. The teacher looked around the room for an escape hatch. His eyes fell on a brother seated in the second row.

"Brother Furbie, could you lead a prayer on this man's behalf? Since we have lost our class time and only have a few minutes until the bell rings us to worship, could you go ahead and lead our closing prayer?" Brother Furbie obliged--as if on cue. Hear his prayer:

"God, we thankest Thou for this time and opportunity to come together to study a portion of Thy Word. We pray that the things that we have partially studied here today will make us a better friend and neighbor. Be with the widows and orphans the world over and the missionaries on foreign fields as they preach Thy gospel to a lost and dying world. Be with us as we enter into the worship portion of this Lord's Day. Give the one who speaks to us today a ready recollection of the things he hath prepared. We pray that the things we do in the exercise of this service will be acceptable in Thy sight. Be with the young man's mother and guide the doctors' hands as they treat her to the best of their ability. Guide, guard and direct us until the next appointed time. We pray this prayer in the name of Jesus, Amen."

The man's eyes were closed so tight and his arms stretched

so high that it felt as if he would need a pry bar to move either set. He didn't want the moment to end, nor did he expect it to so soon. As he lowered his arms, his right arm bumped a woman on the head. She was bending over to gather her purse and Bible from under the seat.

"Oh, I'm sorry," the man exclaimed as he turned to engage her in conversation. The woman simply smiled and quickly moved away, out into the hallway. Others followed the woman quickly out into the hall also. The young man turned to engage the man on his left. He saw an outstretched hand pointing his way. He felt a comfort as he slipped his sweaty, slightly shaking hand into the hand of the Christian next to him.

"Glad you could visit with us today. Come back whenever you get a chance." And then it was over. The visiting man moved toward the teacher. Without so much as an eye contact, the teacher made a lateral pass with the mother's picture, sending the little silver cross onto the floor. Unworded questions began to pour though the man's head at a breakneck pace as he stooped to recover the cross. His heart rate picked up.

"Excuse me," said a feminine voice from behind, "I know a little of what your mother must be feeling. I will pray for your mother." And then with pen and paper in hand, the woman asked, "What is your mother's name? Does she live here in town?"

As the man made his way toward the doorway unhindered, another voice stopped him. "Hey, my mother died from her potassium being too high a couple of years ago. She had a bad adrenalined gland or something. Might be like your mother. I make up the prayer list for the worship service, so if you want I can put your mother's name in there. I'll run it by the Pastor for an OK, but I'm sure that no one will mind."

Giving his mother's name to the prayer scribe was the last order of business in that church. Seeming hundreds of people moving past him to get to the next order of business. A glance, a smile and a bulletin into his hand was all the comfort (and attention) he gathered after the bell rang.

For the next four Sundays, the man did what he had been doing for six weeks to-date: visiting churches and asking for prayers for his mother. Some experiences were mountain tops and some were not. His mind was always torn between his faith in a healing God and the constant nagging worry about what he would need to do with his ailing mother. His father and older sister had been killed in a car accident years ago. His brother flatly refused to do anything in regards to helping with his mother, and his other sister just simply wasn't either reliable enough or financially able to help. He would need to rearrange his house and have a long visit with his own family about the situation.

Time passed. His mother lost weight and fell into depression. The doctors drew blood and sent her for x-rays. She was shuffled between this specialist and that. Then, the son could see that his mother seemed to be turning--for the better.

"We're going to have to assume," said the doctor, "that what you had was a viral infection in your kidneys and adrenal glands, even though the renal biopsy tissue culture came back negative from the lab. I'm going to guess that it was an RNase type virus that would, for sure (the doctor began to talk to a point on the ceiling), decrease enzymatic functions and can give a burst of B-cells making self-reactive immunoglobins-- which are then induced to re-express recombinant activating genes."

The doctor stopped conversing with the ceiling and fixed his eyes back onto the two figures sitting in anticipation of the news, "After ruling out both types of Addison's, or any type of myelogenous cytotoxic dysplasia, we kicked around the idea of doing a second biopsy on the other kidney, but since your November M & C-21 panels came back with some encouraging numbers, we decided that the risk of harm would have been too great. Now it looks like we can probably do a C-7 for a little while and follow this upward progression. You really need to consider stopping smoking, as that never does you any good and will impede your positive progression...."

Blah, blah, blap! Both the mother and her son heard nothing except the words *improvement, encouraging*, and *stopping smoking*. Well, the son heard the last one and the mother shoved it off. Later that night, the man opened his Bible to find the verse in James that told him "The believing-prayer of a righteous person will heal you and Jesus will put you back on your feet." The question of what version he was reading from didn't even cross his mind. All he knew was that the God of the universe had put his mother back on her feet. He knew that it was because he had diligently sought the prayers of those who call on the name of the Lord. He was resolved to say, "Thank you," to those who he had asked to pray. Right then and there he was driven to drop his face to the floor and thank Jehovah God for all He had done.

The teacher was a little nervous as he saw the man once again sitting in the classroom. He knew that the man would have a request, since he was both sitting in the front row of folding chairs and was clutching what appeared to be a 5x7 photograph and a little silver cross in his hand. The teacher decided to get the jump on the man so he wouldn't interrupt during class. After all, he wanted to get through Balak, Baalam, and the talking donkey.

"Good to see you back. We're studying from the Old Testament book of Numbers today. The Old Testament doesn't tell us about salvation, but several New Testament passages tell us that we can learn from the Old Testament nonetheless. Is that a picture of your mother?"

"Yes, I won't take up too much of your time, but I'm going around to all the churches that prayed for my mother. She's doing fine. In fact, (the man was fidgeting around in his chair so much that he almost spun off) she has been going with me but she sprained her ankle on Friday while she was jogging! Jehovah certainly healed my mother because of the intercession prayers of people like you. We're promised that very thing when it says that "If a good man prays for someone they will be healed of their sickness." I read that many times in James! Thanks for all the men and women prayer warriors here at this believer's church. I'm telling all the denominations that we visited (and then he caught himself) but I've already said that. I'm wondering if anyone here can say a praise prayer of jubilee (as he lifted up his hands with palms upward) for my mother? Yes, yes, please praise Father God for following through on his promise to heal Christians like my mother of their illnesses!"

The same eyes of anticipation glowed in the man. The same feeling of eerie stiffness came over the little group of Sunday school members. The man had returned. The rules of church had been rubbed wrongly. The jargon hadn't been used correctly. The Scriptures had been applied wrongly. It was decided individually, inside the members' heads, that this man--and his mother--didn't fit the mold of the New Testament Christian. Sometimes it hurt, but the rules of church would need to be both applied and upheld for the sake of God. It was time to outline very clearly and precisely to this man just how God thinks and operates.

The young man found himself standing outside of the church building.

For over thirty years, for as long as the man had ever known, questions had swirled around in this man's head. He knew what the teachers had told him. He knew that some sin against the God of Israel had been the cause of him not being able to see. He had been reminded of that daily as people would toss copper coins and an occasional piece of silver at his feet while asking him to beg God for forgiveness. He hadn't talked much about it with his parents since he was a teenager. He used to ask over and over who it was that committed this great sin that would so anger God as to have God deprive him of his sight and reduce him to a life of begging alms--if one could call it a life, which it was not.

At least he had a life to live. His parents told him many times about the near death escape they had, narrowly escaping the sword of an enraged King Herod in their little town of Bethlehem. But the little town of Bethlehem wouldn't have done well for the man or any one reduced to begging for that matter. Jerusalem, especially a gate leading into it, caught the best of benevolence. Pilgrims, priests, Levites and businessmen. But now he is used to it: the clanking of the coins, the questions from the little children, and the request of the coin tossers for him to repent.

Today was no different, but it soon would be. The coins and questions still resounded with a sporadic but anticipated clink. This time a question with no coins was involved, but the question wasn't directed to the man on the ground. It was directed to a Rabbi.

"Rabbi, I have a question for you. Take this blind man here in front of us. Would you say that it was his parents or himself that caused the sin that God is punishing. The Rabbi Hillel wrote it was this man's fault, but Rabbi Gamaliel says that can only come from either one of the parents. Which side do you take on this? What is it that we believe on this matter?"

"Well, we were always taught in Synagogue," another man from the group quickly inserted, "that an unborn baby could commit a sin just by being born on the Sabbath, causing the mother to work and break the Sabbath. In that case, both of the senior Rabbis would be right. Am I right? But who would have the greater sin, the mother or the baby? Well, since he's blind, it would be the baby, right?"

There were several "Yep's" and "That's right" and even some strong feelings one way or the other in discussing what God thought. Two men who were probably in the back of the traveling troupe began to argue quite sharply, both equally citing from the Psalms, the Prophets and the Law of Moses.

"Now hold up!"--and they did. This was obviously going to be the Rabbi who would speak next. That coins were not falling at this point didn't bother the blind man. He had enough for the day, though it would be a skinny day. He was more interested in this long tucked away debate. Perhaps another new swirl would be added to his now crowded, yet monotonous head. After all, he had seen the shifting tide of thoughts during his tenure as a coin collector.

"The correct answer is neither Gamaliel's point of view nor Hillel's point of view. This man is blind for this very moment, this very day. It is not that my Father would punish this man for anyone's sins, but in order that the mighty works of God can be displayed in this man through me. This man sees only darkness. Since I am the light of the world, that darkness ends today!"

And then the man spit. Oh yes, he spit. Being blind didn't mean that the man couldn't hear and know what was going on. Dead silence except the shuffling of the feet in order that the companions could get a better view of what was happening. Then the face, the awful feeling of something wet being placed on the man's eyes. He jerked back in both surprise and humiliation as he placed two and two together and realized that this Rabbi was rubbing spit mixed with dirt into his eyes.

Boys will be boys. The man was used to the taunting and rock throwing from little boys, until some kind soul ran them off or otherwise disciplined them. Even then, there were those in the crowd who would find some humor in a blind man being pelted by rocks and the snickers and stifled laughs would soon follow. Well, all in a day's work, but spit! He was just sure that this would be a real crowd pleaser. But no one was laughing. In fact, everyone was silent.

"I'm sending you to the water Sent so you can wash your face. Simon, you and Thaddeus escort our new friend to the pool, but leave him there. He won't need an escort back."

As the two men were pulling up the blind man, the blind man quickly tucked his coins for the day into his pocket. At least he wouldn't lose those. Obviously, the rest of the day would seemingly be a loss. As they traveled, it was apparent that more than Simon and Thaddeus were along for the final humiliation. Not only spit on a blind man, but move him. Now that's original!

"I've seen it all," one said, "Now we're going to get a crowd for sure. He should have never spit on the ground like that and then commenced to make clay. That's two Sabbath rules broken: spitting and making clay."

"Two! Huh, only two? For sure, don't forget application of the clay to this fellow's eyes. Someone could really interpret that as application of some sort of salve or something, and we all know that's forbidden. Man, three fractures of the Law of Moses. I'd follow that man anywhere, but sometimes that Jesus just keeps…"

"Jesus!?" The blind man almost knocked the group to the ground as he ground to a complete halt.

"Heard of him?" one asked.

"Yes, I have. I've heard he is a good man and has the spirit of the prophets of old with him. Yes, yes, I've heard of him. I don't understand why he spit…"

They were there at the water Sent. They helped the man orient himself to the pool's edge and were more than happy to depart as the short walk to the pool had gathered quite a crowd--the very thing these men had come to fear. The man wasted no time in washing the humiliation off his face.

The water was cold, cold enough to sting the eyes and cause the little sparkles of light that dance in one's eyes when there is such a cold substance come in contact with them, like snow during those rare snowfalls in Jerusalem's winters. But this hurt, too. A sharp ray of light seemed to sear through this man's head like a hawk diving for a small animal. He put his hands to his face to feel the damage. None, but some dirt still remained crusted to his eyebrows and lashes. Another splash of water, another shot of light. And then, his hands.

Oh, he knew they were his hands all right. The very hands that had, day after day, remained outstretched as he heard approaching footsteps and conversation from passersby as he began his begging song. They were his, they were attached to his arms, to his shoulders. He put them in the water, then pulled them out. He moved his fingers, then pulled on one finger with the opposite hand. He pulled on his nose, then looked at his beard still draining of water. He lifted his head. For the first time in his life, he was able to put faces to the voices.

Human nature demanded that he return from where he came. He knew that spot. He could find it with his eyes closed. Eyes closed. It hit him like a wall--he blinked, then he blinked again. Then he became fearful of closing his eyes, perchance they would never open again. With drying, stinging eyes, the man returned to his spot only to find no one. No Jesus. He didn't notice the crowd.

Parents pulled their children away. Others came up staring closely into this man's face. Others just stood there in silence. Someone broke that silence. "Who are you?"

Who are you? Funny, no one ever asked him that before. In fact, he can't remember the last time he spoke his own name--but he did. He did again! He walked over to the spot where he had been begging earlier that day, every day, and announced his name with the surname *the blind*, yet he wasn't blind. When asked how this could be, the only thing the man could state was the truth--for to fabricate any explanation now would have just been too much for the man. "The Rabbi Jesus barJoseph spit on the ground, made clay and put it in my eyes.

He told me to wash in the pool Sent and two men or more that were following Jesus helped me over there and I washed and I can see. I don't know what else to tell you. Jesus put clay on my eyes and I can see. I can see. But I can't see Jesus. Is anyone here the Rabbi Jesus? Is the Rabbi Jesus here?"

A feeling of eerie stiffness came over the little group of onlookers. The man had returned to his spot--seeing. The rules of Sabbath had been rubbed wrongly. The jargon hadn't been used correctly. The Scriptures had been applied wrongly. It was decided individually inside the onlookers' heads that this man--and his conclusion--didn't fit the mold of the Law of Moses. Sometimes it hurt, but the rules of Sabbath would need to be both applied and upheld for the sake of God. It was time to outline very clearly and precisely to this man just how God thinks and operates.

It was a matter for the religious leaders. They summoned the so-called man-born-blind-but-now-sees to themselves. Heaven forbid that the shepherds of the sheep would go find him, if for nothing more than sheer curiosity. The man was brought to the religious leaders, clutching a 5x7 picture of his mother and a little silver cross tightly in his hands. His eyes were overflowing with anticipation.

Over and over again the Pharisees were asking him how he received his sight. Each time he said to them, "He applied clay to my eyes, and I washed, and I see." It wouldn't do. No one who was from God would break even the slightest rule from the play book, let alone three rules. It couldn't be. How could someone who wasn't a faithful member in good standing in the little congregation even think that God would heal his mother of an illness. It had to have another explanation.

Maybe the man really wasn't blind. Yes, yes, that must be it! He simply had an eye infection and it got better. Maybe he did a little begging while his vision was impaired. Oh, and by the way, he did mention something about his mother having depression. Maybe she just snapped out of it. The religious leaders have heard of depressed people thinking that they are ill and always going to the doctors. That had to be it.

Therefore, some of the Pharisees were saying, "This man

A Minister's Musing...in Shorts!

is not a New Testament Christian in good standing, because he does not keep the Sabbath." But others were saying (to their own detriment), "How can a man who is a sinner give such glory to God?" And there was a division among them. So a second time they called the man who had been blind, and said to him, "Give glory to God; we know that this man Jesus is a sinner and doesn't follow our rule book on the Law of Moses!"

He therefore answered, "Whether He is a sinner, I do not know. One thing I do know, that, whereas my mother was very sick, and now she is completely well after many prayers from many Christians. I once was blind, but now I see!"

They snapped back to him, nearly screaming with religious rage, "What did He do to you!? How did He open your eyes!? Just how do you think He healed your mother!?"

He answered them, "I told you already, and you did not listen. Why do you want to hear it again? You do not want to become His disciples too, do you?"

And the church leaders reviled him, and said, "You are His disciple, but we are disciples of the restoring movement that put an end to all denominationalism and man-made worship. We know that God has spoken to Moses, but as for this man, we do not know where He is from."

The man answered and said to them, "Well, here is an amazing thing, that you do not know where He is from, and yet He opened my eyes. Your prayer system is weak, with no one really wanting to pray earnestly for my mother's health. You dig in your Bibles and thumb through your scrolls looking for a few words here and there that always seem to say, "NO, no way!" You fidget when someone asks a Christian favor and runs uncomfortably away from anyone on fire for the Lord and His will. A man who was blind and can now see... rocks your boat!"

They answered and said to him, "You were born entirely in sins, and are you teaching us?" And they put him out. John 9:34

Still holding the picture of his mother and twirling the little silver cross on its chain, the man left the church building in a state of confusion. What on earth was that all about? Why were they so angry? What were they so afraid of? Where was the rejoicing and the praise to God? Is that all there is to that group? He found close by a small fountain to sit by and contemplate what had just happened.

Squinting from the bright light of a noonday sun, the man left the council building in a state of confusion. What on earth was that all about? Why were they so angry? What were they so afraid of? Where was the rejoicing and the praise to God? Is that all there is to that group?

The blind man, or so he had been, spots a man about his age sitting by the Pool of Siloam with a most dejected look on his face. Funny, it didn't take long after meeting with the religious leaders to be able to read the facial expressions of people. The man approached the dejected man and asked if he could sit for a while. Without looking each other in the eye, the answer was, "Yes."

"What are you looking at?"

"It's a picture of my mother."

"I'm not familiar with pictures, but I'm familiar with mothers. Is she all right?"

"Oh, yes, she was sick but a man named Jesus...Oh, never mind!" He feels a tightening feeling in his stomach as his heart begins once again to pound. "I don't want to start a fight with you. I don't even know you. What do you do?"

"Well, if you are ready for a story, I don't do anything, I mean, I'm going to have to figure out what I do. You see--see, I'm already saying you see--I used to be a beggar, but the strangest--no, most wonderful thing happened just this morning. You wouldn't believe it, but a fellow named Jesus who is a man about our age came up to me and you would have never guessed that he spit on the ground...

Those of the Pharisees who were with Jesus heard these things, and said to Him, "We are not blind too, are we?" Jesus said to them, "If you were blind, you would have no sin; but since you say, 'We see,' your sin remains." John 9:40f

---

I like happy endings. Too much in the world today doesn't have as such. Let's take another look at the man with the ill mother. Let's put him in a setting that should be. Instead of checking the security of our scripture tassels and digging through our herb pile, let's instead do what Jesus would have done on any given Sabbath:

The Bible class teacher had put weeks worth of work into the lesson. This lesson was pivotal, and was lesson number six of a thirteen week course. The lessons had been printed up for a week. Additional class material had been e-mailed to everyone. Everyone in the Bible class had been studying hard all week. It was for certain that the class could not be covered in one week, and probably could not be covered in two. The teacher had already warned in the e-mail that class would start on time, if not a few minutes early, and distractions would be held to a minimum.

A man came into the Sunday morning Bible class with one thing on his mind: his mother. To be sure, she had not taken care of herself during her fifty-seven years on earth. She had lived it up in the late sixties and early seventies, but that ultimately gave way to simply alcohol and cigarettes, and way too much reliance on over-the-counter remedies of all flavors. However, she was ill. Her son explained that her zyme n' lyte panels didn't look too good, though he neither knew what that meant nor could he produce a number. There was talk of autobodies and syndromes, operations and recoveries, although the young man didn't know what it all meant--and many in the Bible class pretended to by nodding their heads.

All he knew was that his mother was sick and the overall outlook didn't look so well.

He had one request and that was for a prayer of healing for his mother. He knew that he, along with his wife and children, hadn't been to church anywhere on a regular basis, but knew that there was a God in Heaven that both cared and could heal. However, his timing wasn't the best in the world, since he had pretty much blurted out the whole ordeal about his mother during the teacher's lesson, although he believed it was relevant since the class was discussing the bronze serpent in Numbers. Seeing he had the floor, he pulled out a 5x7 picture of his mother and handed it to the teacher.

"If you could please stand my mother's picture up against the teaching stand so everyone can see her...please?" The man had eyes full of both tears and anticipation for what God would shortly do on his mother's behalf. "Thank you, and could you hang this little silver cross over the picture, also? Now my request is that if there is a man or woman here that is one of God's designated prayer warriors, I know that God will hear you since you have the gift of intercession. Who is the designated prayer warrior in this group?"

"I'm one of them," a voice from the back of the room announced, "but I'm nowhere near the only one. If you could be so kind as to give us your mother's name we would be happy, each one of us, to pray on your mother's behalf."

"And we want to pray for you, too," another, softer voice announced. Many of us in this room know how hard it is to be--not the one ill, but--the one having to do."

"After this class, we have a worship time in the main chapel, but if you don't mind, there are several of us that would want to go to your mother's house and have a time of prayer and encouragement with you and her. If that wouldn't be too much of an imposition."

"Enough talk. Let's pass this picture around as I lead us to the throne room of God on behalf of this man's mother. After I'm finished, please, please feel free to jump in…"

God, there's so many things that we don't understand in this life about sickness and pain and hurt, but what we do know right here and now is that there is among us a man whose mother is very ill right now and both mother and son are scared…

Micaiah

Job's wife said to him, "Do you still hold fast your integrity? Curse God and die!" Bildad added, "Lo, God will not reject a man of integrity." And Job quieted them all, "Till I die, I will not put away my integrity from me."

Integrity and truthfulness are cultivated, not hatched for the occasion.

In this day and time it would seem that lying, deceitfulness and guile are commonplace. In fact, we almost expect it when we are out amongst ourselves: grocery store, shopping mall, auto mall, school, work, everywhere. We expect it, and we even rationalize our own use of it. However, we are called to something different, to be someone different. This is the story of one who was different.

While Ahab was not the worst king that the northern ten tribes of Israel had, it would be a monumental mistake to place any redeeming qualities on him. If he wanted something, he would pout and carry on, and then kill to get it. Ahab was on the throne of Israel but he had a throne related problem: he was on the throne of his own life. For the vast part of Ahab's life, God had no anchor in it. It was only when Ahab became confronted with his own mortality that he chose to humble himself before God. It was a short lived humbling, however, and soon he was back to indulging in his old ways. But for a time there was peace, three years of it. Soon that was to end.

There is nothing better than peace, especially when the alternative is war in your own backyard. Peace is a time when a family can be just that--a family, and not have to worry about grabbing their belongings and running for the hills and mountains when the tides of war turn unfavorably on the home front. Peace is a time when children can be children and not have to grow up fast in an adult world of worry, hurt and disappointments. Instead of horror, kids can play in the streets, stomping mud puddles after a summer rain and stirring a stick in the top of an ant bed.

All can enjoy their lives and pursue those things in their lives which bring joy. Mothers can fuss over their son's leaving home to once again start the family process. Fathers can swell with pride as their daughters are given in marriage or their crops and herds are especially noteworthy among the villagers that year. All, young and old alike, can lay their heads down at the end of the day and fully expect to wake up the next morning to pursue life once again.

But there is something about peace which brings about war. It is as elusive as anything in life can be. Peace time to war mayhem. Maybe men get bored. Perhaps egos and pride begin to reign. Perhaps greed is shoved under the noses of people and suddenly their wants turn into that greed. Whatever the answer, nothing has changed in human history in regards to war. We will rationalize, justify, and then summon the troops. It is true today, and was true in the time of King Ahab.

Jehoshaphat ruled in the southern kingdom of Judah. Here was a king that was closer to God than Ahab would ever be. Somewhere in his reign, Jehoshaphat had decided that to serve God, like his ancestor David, was of the highest importance. Throughout the country, idols and shrines to no-gods were torn down. Teachers of the laws of God were dispersed throughout Judah to carry the good news. In fact, the fear of the Lord was even spread to the enemies and neighboring countries surrounding Judah. So much so, in fact, that no one even dared think of invading Judah.

However, all men make poor choices in life. Some have little consequences, the result lasting only a few minutes. Other choices tend to change the course of life and history. Jehoshaphat was no exception in the scheme of humanity. However it came about, he decided to ally himself with King Ahab through marriage. It is because of this alliance that the two kings found themselves together, seated on their thrones, at the gates of the capital city of Israel, the city of Samaria.

A Minister's Musing...in Shorts!

The fanfare was enormous. Both kings were sitting on their thrones in full display of the citizens of Samaria. The smell of roasting animals filled the air as one of the greatest parties that Samaria had seen in years was well under way. Thoughts and talk raced through the city as folks wondered whether or not this would be the beginning of a unified twelve tribes once again. If not unification, then maybe this was a sign of a long peace between Israel and Judah. Either way, tensions were abated for the time being and the festivities were in full bloom. The stage was set and the trap was ready to be sprung. Little did the godly King Jehoshaphat know that his visit to his neighbor to the north was to soon to play into the selfish wants of King Ahab.

Jehoshaphat was rich. Real rich. But along with his wealth came respect, the kind of respect from his countrymen that would cause them to follow the good king anywhere. Did he want a building program? Then they would build for him. Did the king want all the kingdom to listen to the Law of the Lord as traveling priests and prophets went throughout the country reading from the Book? Then they would listen and learn. Did king Jehoshaphat want a large standing army? Then he would have it. Did he want that army to fight? Fight they would...and Ahab knew it!

The side conversations and murmuring had been going on ever since Jehoshaphat arrived in the capitol city of Israel. Ahab would pause and speak to his trusted advisors and assemblage that always seemed to be close at hand. Small comments exchanged between them that were accompanied by frowns and other signs of great concern. Jehoshaphat would inquire if everything were all right, only to be answered that they were, but the look on Ahab's face would insist that they weren't. The trigger on the trap was ever so close to being pulled. For Ahab, this was the end of act one.

The wining and dining continued. The festivities intensified. Hordes of people came by to pay their respects to the two sovereigns, wondering what it must all be about. The side conversations continued between Ahab and his cronies. Again Jehoshaphat asked if everything were fine. This time he got an answer, and it would be an answer that one of them couldn't live with: Ramoth-Gilead belonged to Israel and it was time to take it back.

Twenty five miles or so southeast of the Sea of Galilee, the city state of Ramoth-Gilead had been in the original land that the half tribe of Manasseh had settled east of the Jordan River. The strategic importance of Ramoth-Gilead was recognized when King Solomon made the town a post for one of his twelve deputies during his reign. Slowly, as Syria crept closer to the Jordan River, Ramoth-Gilead had been swallowed up and out of the hands of Israel. Though peace had reigned for three years, Ahab decided it was time to take it back. The more help he could muster, the better.

Jehoshaphat was skeptical. He knew what Ahab and Jezebel were about, and they weren't about Jehovah God. Baal worship in the northern kingdom of Israel had long been entrenched as the state religion. Ahab and Jezebel both had gone out of their way to avoid God. Except for Ahab's repenting before God to spare his life just a few years earlier, the godless couple had gone out of their way to thwart the efforts of the prophet Elijah and a call of repentance not just for the king and queen, but also for the entire nation of Israel. Though Jehoshaphat initially pledged his allegiance to Ahab, he had another allegiance and that was Jehovah God. He wouldn't budge unless the Lord told him that war was the answer. The 'answer' was already assembled around the two thrones in the form of four hundred prophets whose entire existence was one of satiating King Ahab.

Mankind wants to hear good things especially when the good things concern self. It is one of the oldest traps that mankind can fall into. Indeed, the lie that we will 'be like God' was among the first traps set for us as a race in the Garden of Eden. It has, and will continue to be, a snare for man. Deep down inside Ahab knew that the four hundred prophets carrying on and kicking up dust in front of him with shouts of, "Go up to Ramoth-Gilead, for the Lord will give it to you," was just so much pump and pomp. Jehoshaphat knew it too. Ahab was set on seeking a strong answer of affirmation from Jehoshaphat and wouldn't stop until he got it. He was on the verge until Jehoshaphat made his final request: "Was there

A Minister's Musing...in Shorts!

not a true prophet of the Lord left in all of Samaria that would tell it like it was?"

Ahab was stuck. His plan began to show holes in it. Four hundred uniformly favorable prophets were not enough. Jehoshaphat had begun to see the prophets for what they really were and Ahab knew it: yes men. With his mind ever turning, Ahab relented and spoke of one remaining prophet in town, and that was Micaiah. But Micaiah's name came with a warning label: Jehoshaphat shouldn't put too much emphasis on what this prophet had to say, for the prophet Micaiah never had anything good to say about Ahab. Jehoshaphat knew that this was the one that needed consulting, and insisted.

When folks have a free ride in life, when easy street is an everyday occurrence, they will generally do anything that they can to keep that particular street open. The four hundred prophets were no exception. They had enjoyed, perhaps, years of simply keeping King Ahab in the feel good side of life. They weren't about to let that slip away by the requests of a visiting king. As soon as the order was given to bring Micaiah to the kings' presence, one of the false prophets, Zedekiah, sprung into action. Iron horns were gathered as quickly as they could be had. Imitating a bull, Zedekiah began snorting and kicking up dust as a raging bull would in the presence of a threat. With the iron horns firmly held to the side of his head, he assured the kings that if they would but simply head into the direction of Syria, the Syrians would surely fall by the wayside.

We find Micaiah detained by Amon, the governor of the capitol city. We have no reason to believe he is held in prison, just simply detained--and out of the way. Ahab wasn't about to allow Micaiah to roam free in the city of Samaria, for Ahab knew that Micaiah would have long presented himself in the city's festivities and begun his line of prophecy warning Jehoshaphat before Ahab could set his plan in motion. Now, Ahab had no choice but to rely on sheer numbers to persuade Judah's king to join him in battle. The unnamed messenger arrived at Micaiah's holding spot. In his hand was a letter from Ahab. In his mouth was a warning to Micaiah.

The messenger was concerned for Micaiah's safety. For too many long years he had been first hand witness to Ahab's way of carrying out judgment on those who either undermined him or simply got in his way. The incident of Naboth's vineyard, and the dead body that incident produced, was as fresh on the mind of the messenger as if it had happened only yesterday. He had one warning to Micaiah, and that was to play along. The so-called prophets were united in their efforts to tell Ahab what he wanted to hear. All Micaiah had to do was join them, to bring the total of yes-sayers to four hundred and one. It would be easy, quick, and no doubt Micaiah could go on his way at that point. However, Micaiah was not only a man of integrity and truthfulness, he was a man committed to God.

Integrity and truthfulness are cultivated, not hatched for the occasion.

It was Micaiah's way of life to tell, as we say, the truth, the whole truth and nothing but the truth. That way of life must be in place before the moment arises. Once the moment arises, it is often too late to decide to become a man of integrity. Integrity and truthfulness must be an integral part of a man's life if it is to come forth during difficult and stressful times. Micaiah's answer was clear: He would speak only as God directed him.

No one knows the reaction of the messenger that summoned Micaiah from his state of holding. We do not know if Micaiah was someone that he looked up to or otherwise had a fondness for. Perhaps summoning the prophet was all in a day's work, and he simply wanted things at the presence of the king to go smoothly. Maybe the messenger was caught up in the now brewing fervor of a 'glorious little war' to take back part of an earlier Israel. Whatever the intent of asking Micaiah to go along with the other so-called prophets, the messenger now leaves the picture. The picture changes as Micaiah now stands before Ahab and Jehoshaphat. Ahab has one question to ask Micaiah: Do Israel and Judah combine forces and jointly attack the Syrians and take back Ramoth-Gilead, or do they simply put up with the present state of affairs?

The moment was both tense and quiet. For the time being, the four hundred prophets had ceased their carrying on. Zedekiah quietly removed the iron horns from his temples and stopped kicking up dust. King Jehoshaphat leaned forward intently anticipating Micaiah's response, somehow knowing that this man would speak for God, regardless of Ahab's wishes and desires. Ahab sat back on his throne, mouth held sideways and eyes turned upward like a man who is expecting his prediction to come true. As Micaiah opened his mouth to speak, Ahab shifted a little on his throne.

Inevitability, especially when the outcome is not personally favorable, has a tendency to give birth to sarcasm. A man who feels that all he has, and all that he is, is about to be stripped will resort to sarcasm. It is a survival mechanism that helps overcome the pain and disappointment of that inevitability. It is the old "if I'm going out, I might as well have some fun with this thing." Micaiah was up for a little fun, if only for the sake of being able to remember Ahab's frustration, fear and facial expressions long after the inevitable had come to be. Micaiah's 'prophecy' was in. It was the 'assurance' that the king of Israel need only head off into battle and the Lord God would deliver Ramoth-Gilead into his hands.

Perhaps it was the wildly exaggerated way in which Micaiah delivered his verdict. Maybe it was the hand gestures along with the facial expressions. Perhaps it was the slight upturn in the way Micaiah ended his statement, a sort of question leaving a question mark about the whole affair. Whatever it was, Micaiah got his point across. That point was this: thoughts of battle needed to be shelved. It would not go well for Israel, for God would bless no such endeavor. Ahab knew it. He knew it all along. One can almost hear Ahab begin to rant and rave.

"I knew it! I knew it! Did you hear what he said? I told you he never has anything good to say about me! Now he is simply trying to make sport of me, mocking me in front of YOU, the king of all Judah, and in front of all of my trustworthy prophets of Jehovah God that have been telling me to go up to Ramoth-Gilead, --*blah, blah, blah*," and so it went as King Ahab tried to right the situation, tipping it back into his favor. Then, Ahab turned his attention back to Micaiah.

"How many times must I adjure you to speak to me nothing but the truth in the name of the Lord?" And so, Micaiah did. He flat out stated that if Ahab goes to war, he will not be coming back. "See," Ahab told Jehoshaphat, "I told you he never has anything good to say about me. This is why

I didn't want to bring him here, he's always talking down to me..."

Micaiah didn't let him finish. He went on to prophecy that God was the one beefing up these four hundred so-called prophets. God was the one enticing Ahab to go up against Ramoth-Gilead. Let's look at this realistically. Who says that God doesn't have a sense of humor? Here is a king literally hell-bent on doing evil and doing things his way, and anyway but God's way and God is having a little fun with Ahab's self-centeredness! It is ever true that God eventually gives mankind what he wants: Heaven or Hell.

Micaiah's story begins to end here. We can only guess at the ending, since he is spoken of no more in Scripture. Zedekiah drops the iron horns on the ground and pops Micaiah across the mouth. Micaiah tells Zedekiah to watch it, and then adds that Zedekiah has no idea what is coming down the pike. Ahab has enough and tells the guards to throw Micaiah in prison. Not just in prison, but to be fed sparingly with bread and water until the king returns. Got that? *Until the king returns!*

Ahab didn't. Not upright in his chariot, anyway. Ahab returned to Samaria crumpled in the blood covered floor of his chariot, a single arrow protruding from his chest. After they buried King Ahab, they took his chariot to a side pool that the whores used to bathe. They couldn't get the chariot washed fast enough. The local dogs kept licking the blood out of the chariot floor.

Now, here's the lesson. It's not a question of whether or not you are an Ahab. That question doesn't apply, for there won't be any Ahabs reading this in the first place. The question is whether or not you are a Micaiah.

Micaiah was no dummy. He knew the score when Ahab told the guards to toss Micaiah into the prison on a bread and water ration until the king's return. He knew Ahab wouldn't come back. He knew he would never get out of prison--alive. He knew there would be long days as intense hunger and thirst would slowly overwhelm him. He would not be familiar with the term catabolysis, but would fall to it. His dry throat would be overtaken with a painful fungal overgrowth as he began to hallucinate and become unable to move. He would shiver as he lay in his own filth.

He would cry out to God with questions that would only, and could only, be answered after his death.

A bunch of folks are standing around the water cooler or in the lunchroom at work. You walk by. One says with a chuckle in his voice, "Hey, Fred, are you one of those Bible believers? Huh?" You say, "Yes, I am." You feel good about having stood up for Jesus. Now, another time and another place, your door is smashed at four in the morning. You've already heard the sporadic gunfire up and down the street. The three men and two dogs pull you and your spouse from your bed and want to know if you are Christians or not. Yes, or no. They are pulling hard on your hair and have already shoved a pistol in your eye socket so hard that it causes searing pain. Your children are screaming. Your spouse is clutching your arm so hard it has already started tingling from lack of blood.

But that time is yet for the future. Or was that in mankind's past somewhere? We look, and we see integrity under fire throughout our timeline on earth.

A small woman, a foreigner, a missionary, stood her ground in China in the 1930's. Behind her were dozens of frightened Chinese orphans. In front of her were blood-crazed Japanese Imperial soldiers armed with Arisaka rifles tipped with sixteen inch bayonets. These soldiers had already been rampaging through China for over a year. Hundreds of thousands of Chinese men, women and children had already been murdered: bludgeoned, bayonetted, blown up or burned. Thousands upon thousands of women and young girls had already been brutally raped.

The Imperial soldiers now wanted the children, to rid the land of vermin. The missionary was free to go. A translator among the soldiers made his request--demands--perfectly clear. Bayonets were leveled at the intended victims.

In clear and concise Mandarin Chinese, as she pulled herself upright and steadfast in front of the children, the missionary told them, "No!"

Integrity and truthfulness are cultivated, not hatched for the occasion.

King of Burns

*Leave the presence of a fool, or you will not
discern words of knowledge.
A fool does not delight in understanding,
but only in revealing his own mind.*

A Couple of Solomon's Proverbs

Some people run all their lives trying to figure out what to be when they grow up. Sadly, I have fallen into that quest over the last fifty-something years. I have been everything under the sun for at least five minutes or ten years--you take your pick. Sometimes I've been at the right place at the right time, tickling the right person. I've drilled gas wells in the canyon lands of Utah. I've drilled oil wells in the deserts of New Mexico. I've drilled dry wells all over. I have preached, pastored, policed, painted and poked people with needles. I tested the soil percolation rate and--for a brief moment in the 70's--held the power to pass or fail the entire Dallas-Ft. Worth Airport's Phase II expansion project. Well, at least it felt like I had that kind of power.

No one has that kind of power.

Sometimes I've been--not so much in the wrong place at the wrong time scenario--just nothing. Take houses for instance. I've bought four houses in my life. The very first house I owned, I bought for $33,000 and sold for $30,000 with some structural damage compliments of the Balcones Fault. No, it wasn't a typo: buy $33K. Sell $30K. Ugh! The second house I bought for $74,900 and sold for $37,500 (yes folks, 50¢ on the dollar) some eight years later due to the falling of crude oil prices and the dismemberment of a town in Nowhere, New Mexico. Third house I bought for $110K and don't want to talk about it. I'm currently living in the fourth. We'll see. Funny, though, that the sizes of the houses don't change appreciably. Only the cost does.

I have extra skin on my body. No need to discuss just where, but it seems as if there is some sort of design flaw at work here. People don't need extra skin. I don't want to grow into it. I just don't need it but Goodwill won't take it. I thought about listing the extra skin on Craigslist, but I have been told not to bother. I get told a lot of things.

I don't control anything or anyone. I'm not in charge of anything or anyone. We're empty nesters, but my children check up on me 'just because.' I bought a new home entertainment setup--and had to have someone set it up. My pharmacist recognizes the front of my vehicle in the drive-up window and has my monthly drugs ready for me. I'm told that if I do not take these drugs that I will simply just cease to exist.

With a little bit of reworking, I have just described every fifty-something year old married male's life. There is a time when we sit back, examine our gray hair (or scalp, whichever applies) and our built in TV tray and wonder what the heck is going on and where did we get off and why aren't the babes staring at us anymore? Actually, they are staring, but they have their mouths open, there eyes are really wide and they're saying things like, "Oh, my gosh..."

We're reminded every morning when our ankles hit the floor that the clock is ticking. Didn't say that we are headed for the wheel chair or the glue factory. Just simply that those first few steps toward the bathroom every morning take concentration. Not real sure what is the precise age that one notices that their body isn't quite what it was in high school. Probably a much higher age for men than women, but we're off the track here. In fact, it has only been in the last week or two that I noticed that my body was not the same body that I had in high school when I was running track. Or it may have something to do with mothballs.

I pulled my Boy Scout uniform out of the cedar chest the other day to try it on. I last removed it from my body when I was seventeen. Well, maybe I was just still pumped up from the gym when I tried it on. Anyway, it didn't fit well. No, it didn't fit at all.

It really didn't.

And that caused me to drift back to those thrilling days of yesteryear. Me and my extra hide are sitting in my naugahyde chair and I'm immediately transformed to a family vacation when we still had two-thirds of the children still at home. Soon I'm not sitting in my naugahyde seat, but the driver's seat as we are packed up and heading out on an adventure...

...I am currently on vacation with the fam. We are attempting to cover a gozillion miles again. Just remembered that this is something that we said that we would never do again, after taking a monumental trip from West Texas to Traverse City, Michigan via the pothole capitol of America--Columbus, Ohio. I guess that we just forgot and booked another long excursion. The first stop was LaPine, Oregon for a few days camping, which is some of the best camping in Oregon. Then a giant leap from Central Oregon to some lake on the Utah, Idaho and almost Wyoming border. We never really made that lake, even after a fifteen hour run. The mountain was on fire when we got there so we had to get a room in Logan, Utah. Actually, it wasn't a bad room at $60 per night with cable, indoor pool and continental breakfast. I know what some of you are thinking--*now THIS is camping at its finest!*

That first continental breakfast morning I had massive amounts of lobby coffee and some Danishes that I couldn't pronounce the name of if I saw them written down. Aren't we funny people when we're on the road? These were 'Haagan Streus Bavarian Pastries' if I recall anything. We get all warm and giggly inside, thinking that we are somehow on the banks of some river in Denmark, eyeballing copper statues of antiquity and living the good life. Reality demands that these funny named donuts were probably fried down the street by an overweight college student named Stan. I did have a brief conversation with another fancy pastry eater. He asked me if I was married. I said, of course, yes and that my wife was an angel. He just shook his head as he slowly hung it downward and said that I was lucky, that his wife was still alive. OK, conversation was dull, however, the pastries were good and I grazed mightily.

I usually just call them fancy donuts, which reminds me of a long stretch of Idaho interstate ("How'd he do that?!"). Now the speed limit was (and still is two days later, I'm sure) 75 miles per hour. There was this Idaho State Police car doing--you guessed it--72 miles per hour. No one wanted to pass him for fear of being shot on site or whatever goes through people's minds when faced with that situation. We finally dug and dug into the little compartment between the front bucket seats (what DO you call that little compartment?) and came up with a donut call. Neat little thing that sounds like a wounded donut. Dunkin' Donuts used to pass these out for free in boxes of donut holes back when I was in college. I just managed to hang onto mine, like I hung onto my Diving Tony the Tiger action figurine (yell, "Aroogah!" if you still have your Diving Tony).

So there we are in the middle of Idaho, which is the middle of nowhere. Trust me on that one. We roll down the window and let the 72 mph wind blow that thing long and loud. There was a momentary slowdown of the policeman to about 67 mph as he rolled his window down, straining to listen with his head cocked out of the window. This angered the folks around us, but we knew where this was going. Sometimes in life you have to take the bad with the good. We blew it again and I'll be darned if he didn't just leave the roadway into open range land. Works every time. Bet he's still out there:

"Unit nine to base."

"Come in unit nine, this is base."

"I'm exiting the Interstate at mile 127 East in pursuit."

"Unit nine, there is no exit there, come back."

"Unit nine to base. There is now."

"Unit nine, do you require backup?."

"No. Base, I repeat, no! Especially not Charlie."

"Unit nine, are you on foot? Again, unit nine, are you on foot?"

"Are you kidding?"

Anyway, all of this is *certainly* leading up to the problem of being fifty-something and wondering what to do with the rest of one's life ("How? I can't follow this guy..."). Most of the folks in this world are probably not opportunists. In reality, opportunities pass us by at the rate of whatever, and we simply nod at them and wonder 'what if' till that thought is replaced by something else. Then we get with our friends and start a conversation with, "You know, what I'd like to do is..." If you stop and think about it too hard, it is probably a sad thing. Well, we end up doing something. We also gather up mortgages, car payments, orthodontist payments and enough stuff around our houses to hold a garage sale every weekend for the months of September and October.

So that brings us to the part where we were driving along in Eastern Oregon ("Did he just shift gears again?"). Now that is a place that you either have to love, or have to hope that someone else is driving while going through so that you can wash down massive amounts of barbiturates and sleep. The latter will see it as dry, unpopulated with people, animals and plants. I figure that this is the majority of people for there aren't any people out in Eastern Oregon. Animals and plants feel the same way.

I am the former group. At every turn, dip and bend in the road I was squealing like a three year old on Christmas morning. "Look at that! Will you just look at THAT?! Get a load out that window!" As we approached Burns, Oregon the squealing stopped and was replaced by a discussion of just how big a town was Burns. I may have lost that discussion, but that's not important right now.

Burns has no real suburbs, but a distinctive downtown area. The old kind that reminds one of a cross between the wild west, the Great Depression and the current depression. Not that we're in a depression, but it seemed that Burns was.

Suddenly it hit me as I was watching absolutely nothing going on in the streets of Burns. Simply put, they need a king. No, seriously, a king. I looked at a map and figured that a town that is where Burns is, probably doesn't know what is going on in the state, much less the nation. I would simply just stop, put a folding chair down in the middle of city center and put a sign up that says 'King.' Then, I would enlist the help of my family (who would greatly benefit from my being king)

A Minister's Musing...in Shorts!

to move in and among the Burnsians to answer any questions they may have.

"Just what does that ol' boy think he is, a-sittin' on that lawn chair down town?"

"He is the king," my ardent supporters (consisting, at first, entirely of my immediate family and a few close friends) would say.

"But we don't need no stinking king," I can imagine would be the immediate, uneducated reply.

Those same ardent supporters would ardently reply, "It's OK, he's just the king."

Pretty soon folks in Burns would slowly soften up to the idea of having a king. I would become familiar. Familiarity has her place and does her work. When something becomes familiar enough, it soon becomes expected. When it is gone, it is missed. A little like the liberation of some of the death camps after the second world war: the gates were opened and the prisoners slowly shuffled back to their bunkhouses after seeing what all the commotion was. Tragic as the death camps were, they were now familiar surroundings with all the Pavlovian trappings.

Now I'm not comparing Burns to a death camp at all, however, there are a few things that I would have to change in Burns after I became king. Mind you, I didn't have a whole lot of time to do the full scale study that I would normally do in these circumstances. After all, except for one light (I think that there was a light in city center somewhere) it was pretty much a 35 mph trip through the town. Anyway, there is a trailer park at the end of town that also has a big sign up welcoming RV's. That will have to go.

To be certain, I don't have anything against trailer houses. I've lived in bunches of them while drilling for that oil and gas I mentioned earlier. We even lived in one while going to seminary. It was a good little trailer (16x80 if my blocked out memory serves me at all) sitting off on the edge of town--such as town was. There was plenty of sand surrounding us and a few peach trees on the lot. That was years ago, so the peach trees are probably paying off now.

We lived there for one and a half years and went through three hot water heaters and two air conditioners. The front porch was dry rotted so we were forced to just use the back door which was convenient enough since we parked there. I don't ever remember anyone coming around to the front door and knocking--but then again, I never remember looking under the front porch to see if anyone had fallen through. It was one of those back door houses like a lot of grandparents of the past had.

But the RV part of the park in Burns somehow rubbed me the wrong way. Impressions are everything when one is doing a fly-through on a king scouting trip. Maybe I'm prejudiced against RV's. I prefer a pop-up tent trailer myself. Outside of Burns somewhere in that vast expanse known as Eastern Oregon we came across an RV in a ditch.

No, it wasn't a ditch, it was a twenty foot drop off. Maybe thirty. The RV--motor home type which resembled a Greyhound bus--was upright, but drastically lower than the road. Looked as if everyone was OK, but we spent the next hour trying to figure out just how it got down there and also what everyone must have been thinking during that three to four seconds of silence as it flew through the air. I'm pretty sure, human nature being what it is, that the driver was feverishly pumping the brakes in an attempt to stop this thing in mid-flight. I'm just as sure that whoever was sitting in the front passenger's seat during that fly over was frantically giving last minute advice about turning the wheel and slowing down.

Maybe I spent too many years backpacking the remote regions of the Trans-Pecos area of Texas and in the Rocky Mountains of New Mexico. When you start out there, it is hard to understand a traveling motor-show that is bigger than some folks' apartments that I know. But I am a diehard loyalist to certain brands, things and ideas. If there were suddenly no Fords, I would walk. If Apple leaves, I will switch over to a Big Chief tablet and write. No Briggs & Stratton? I'll purchase a sickle and some goats to do the lawn. Besides that, I never quite understood people with travel trailers and big buses. The more gadgets and gizmos it has, the prouder folks are of it. The more it resembles their homes that they are desperately trying to get away from for a week or two, the better it is. Listen to the bragging. Maybe deep down inside we don't want to leave the safety of our homes and venture out very far into the great unknown. RV's are like turtle shells.

I'm not so sure that I saw any fast food restaurants in Burns. Maybe there are, but I don't remember them. As king of Burns I think that I would either oust them or forbid them, whichever applies. I am sure that there is a little restaurant in Burns that the locals go to and it is just fine. No need to mess with just fine. Somewhere there the waitresses call you 'Hon' and keeps your coffee filled. Somewhere there is a menu that you can order off of with a little dignity.

One can simply ask for a cheeseburger and not have to call it 'Slim's Belly Bonanza.' It is a place where you can order an ice cream sundae to top it off and not have someone rush a paper pirate hat onto your head while the hired help comes out dressed as parrots, flapping their arms, all the while squawking a zany song at you. Since this culinary dignity is what is needed in the new Kingdom of Burns (and needed everywhere, wouldn't you agree?) I'll preserve it with ferocity, or create it, which will boost my stock in this king thing anyway.

Now in case you didn't pick up on it, I'm not big on the fast food. I have a tough time matching wrapped and squashed burgers with the word RESTAURANT. I have an even harder time reconciling a drive up window with the word DINING. However, as we traveled through Utah we did break down and stop at one of these things. I hesitate to name the chain, since I do not condone, so I will not mention clowns and arches or anything else that would give you so much as a clue--and cause me some type of retribution in my endeavor to write.

While munching on the wrapped bunned item I was forced to buy and eat for self-preservation, I could see straight into the small kid's play area. You know, the one with the twist and turn tubes. No matter how they arrange the thing it always ends up in a pile of multicolored balls. There must have been nearly a hundred or more small children flailing around in the pile and twisting through the colored tunnels. Meanwhile, there were half a dozen moms stirring about of all shapes and sizes. All had on stretch pants. I was told by a wise woman once that there are two types of women who shouldn't wear stretch pants: those who don't look good in them, and those who do! This particular scene held both.

Anyway, these moms all had something more in common than stretch pants: they were stressed out. They were peering in the balls looking for their children as if there might be some trap door under the balls. They hovered and tippy-toed to look in the tubes as if there might be an ugly troll exacting a toll of children somewhere in there. They would momentarily back off and go to the table and rearrange the untouched food. Every few minutes one of the little ones would emerge from the ball jungle and head to the table for a quick drink and to shove a fry or two into their gullets. After these children, who barely stood above the height of the table finished snacking, Stress Moms would chase them back into the ball abyss with a napkin, but to no avail.

I'm sure that there was a smell thing going on somewhere in there that was stronger than the smell of the wrapped burgers and fries. To me all the children looked alike (and I already mentioned the moms) and all the children were too short to knock their heads back and look at moms with any perspective of detail, so it had to be the smell. Or perhaps when Stress Moms place their children in a commons it becomes any available mom's duty to chase them with a napkin. I honestly don't know.

As I watched this ritual I noticed that there was a serious lack of males in the ball area. I looked scrutinizingly at the door for a sign forbidding males from entering. Perhaps, since we were in Utah, it was an unwritten code that was simply understood--males must avoid the ball area. So what does one do if he is a male and forbidden in the ball zone? As we choked down the rest of our wrapped specimens with carbonated water bought at a ridiculous price, I began to notice that the other males were doing the same. In fact, since they had time to kill (of which I didn't, needing to return to the road) they were reduced to reading the paper and staring out into the parking lot and beyond. The ball ritual is too much for me and too segregating, so I will keep the number of fast food joints to zero in Burns.

Clutter is another thing that would not be allowed in Burns. I'm not against rich or poor either one (though I prefer to be the former), but not big on clutter. Any rung on the socioeconomic ladder can produce clutter. It simply wouldn't be allowed in yards after I become King of Burns, Oregon. I did worry about this, since on the trip we looked as if we ought to be serenaded by the theme to the Beverly Hillbillies as we drove down the highways and byways. The pickup truck with a thousand items in the back, all tied down with rope and blue tarp. It became a game to see if we could find someone--some poor family--that looked more like a traveling junk yard than we did. My wife assured me that since this was summer that we wouldn't be two-hundred yards down the road before we spotted a winner.

Hundreds of miles and days later we still hadn't spotted anyone as a winner and it looked as if we would be the wieners. Now mind you that everything was packed decently and in order. The stacking and packing was engineered with precision. Weight was balanced. Stretch cords were utilized. A mile down the road I stopped and checked to see if everything was riding well. Many of you men reading this are, I'm sure, nodding your heads in approval. We *looked* junky, but we were precise. More precise than the family in Salt Lake City. Or should I say traveling through Salt Lake City.

I swerved on the interstate to avoid a purple something that looked unmistakably like one of the giant Tupperware packing devices that we were using several of. Not a hundred yards down the road there was an SUV pulled over with a matching giant purple Tupperware packing device on top and an unmistakable blank spot where another one should be. A Stress Mom and a Mad Dad occupied the vehicle. I knew immediately that he had broken the engineer/drive a mile/check rule. We imagined that the conversation went something like this:

"I specifically ASKED you if that stuff would ride on the top and you said that it would, no problem, and now what are we going to do and which Tupperware was it that fell off and you'll have to go get it off this very busy freeway in the middle of Salt Lake City during rush hour traffic and whichever container it is, it is more important than your safety at this point and if you get run over and spread out from exit 17 to

23 it is no concern of mine because I can get another husband right back there at that last town and . . ."

"Blah, blah, excuses, blap. . . and you packed the TRAVELER'S CHECQUES and EXTRA CASH in that tub?!?!?"

As tragic as that was for that family, and especially for the male, they weren't cluttered like we were. We still looked for the winner to remove us from the wiener list. After dropping Mom off at a ski resort for a work related 'conference' and getting back on the road (what kind of a deal is that?) me 'n the boys found our match. Whoever you are, you win.

There it was, a station wagon packed to the gills inside with all sorts of baby paraphernalia such as strollers and those things you put kids in so they can roll around in the kitchen while you are carrying hot pots of boiling water and pans of sizzling grease. Behind the station wagon, they were towing a rented trailer. Now that in itself was not grounds for winning. Even adding the fact that they had travel bags strapped to the top wasn't enough to win. The winning blow came with the laundry basket strapped on top. Not a laundry basket full of dirty clothes, but an empty one. Blue, I believe, but once again, just a plain dime store type of everyday laundry basket. Again, we imagined the conversation as the station wagon was ready to embark on its journey from somewhere to newwhere:

"Well, I believe we are packed up and ready to go. I've over-engineered this thing and have everything we need at every stop readily accessible. I drove by the weigh station down the road for an overload check. I even drove it around the block (both directions) at a high rate of speed to check the tethering on the load. While driving it around the block I had all of my manly male friends come out and ooh and aah at the swell job I did distributing the load, taking into account everyone's body weight and did I forgot to tell you that the family has assigned seating to ensure load distribution on the shock absorbers and…"

"You forgot this laundry basket."

"Throw that @%#&! thing away. I don't have it in my master uni-track plan."

"This is a brand new laundry basket! Do you know how much these things cost? You knew that I had to do laundry before we left with these thousand babies we have! What do you mean throw it away?! There's something that needs throwing away around here and it isn't the laundry basket!"

Anyway, they won hands down. The final straw was when we passed him and I sort of gave that road nod and a flick of the hand. He desperately wanted to be somewhere else with that laundry basket strapped on top. He had been made by another male. In short, busted. If he hadn't been in the middle of nowhere, he would have stopped at a dime store and purchased one of those glasses and mustache disguise kits and worn it. As king, and a fellow male, I understand these predicaments. It is ugly, and tears away at the very fabric of maleness across this country.

The wife was quietly curled up in the passenger seat reading a book as we passed. She had her laundry basket.

There was a close second to the laundry basket vehicle. This was a rusty, sputtering car with Oregon plates. I don't have anything against rusty, sputtering cars. Drove an old '64 F-100 pickup like that once. Don't have anything against being from Oregon. Lived there once, too. Each person must drive what they drive, however, it was packed to the hilt and had a sofa strapped on top. A sofa. Not a lazy boy type overstuffed chair, but a whole sofa. A fraying blue tarp (which is, incidentally, the Oregon state flag) attempted to cover it. Only a wave of sympathy for a fellow Oregonian kept it at number two. As loaded down as we were, we had no trouble passing it up.

So, clutter in Burns would not be allowed. They can keep any toilets used as flower pots in the yards, but must have geraniums only and no weeds. They must have no cracks in the porcelain. All cracks in paved driveways must be void of weeds, also.

As opposed to the Willamette Valley (the green and wet part of Oregon) where swimming is an indoor sport, Burns seems to me to be a great spot to swim. As of yet, I do not know if there is a swimming pool in Burns--or even so much as a mud hole to wet oneself in, but since I have declared myself King of Burns I will busily set out to establish a pool. Of course there will be restrictions at this pool: everyone must keep their clothes on.

I didn't think that this was something that had to be

spelled out to a Post Modern Twenty-first century pool goer until we landed in Utah at a resort campground. Now mind you, there are many folks from other countries that will do the National Park circuit each summer. Folks from Holland, Germany, Switzerland and Austria to name a few. Probably they have a different bathing suit standard than we do. In fact, the same amount of material that we would put into the making of an American place mat, they can utilize for at least two adult female swim suits and enough left over for one man's swim suit.

Now from what I could gather, these tiny swim suits must be irritating to the body. While thrashing about this resort pool with the youngest (my middle child was back at camp roasting a chipmunk), I noticed these two women suddenly sat up from their roasting positions and began to chatter amongst themselves as they both began to rummage about in one of those obligatory bags that women must carry to the pool (I've often wanted to peek inside one of those bags). I thought it odd that they both felt the need to rummage and chatter at the same time, so I continued to watch, purely out of cultural interest.

They were pulling something out of the bag that was smaller than their hands, so I couldn't make out what it was. Then they both proceeded to stuff whatever these yet undetermined items were into their very small tops (material wise). Then in a choreographed motion, off came the tops to reveal small pasties and back down on the roasting pads front side up so as to gather the maximum from the sun.

I can only guess that before the idea of a band-aid hit them for the southern regions, the manager arrived on the scene. Now here is where the fun began. Here is an American male who is desperately trying (or so it seemed) to convince two non-American women that roasting with pasties in public is not American. It may be non-American, but is not American. Lots of pantomiming. Lots of teen boys stumbling over one another as they suddenly remembered that they needed something-- ANYTHING-from the other side of the pool. In Burns, I will have signs up in English, Spanish, Dutch and German (for starters) explaining that there will be no incidences akin to this one. I can only guess that the majority of the population of

Burns, Oregon will agree with me after I am familiarized into their town.

Here it is, a summer--no, many--later, and I'm bummed. No so much as a 'hail' has been heard from Burns, Oregon on this king thing. Timing? Timing is right for I am currently unemployed and have half the house packed up and nowhere to go.

People let opportunities pass them by, but I'm convinced that towns and cities do to. Town fathers wrestle with interests and egos, while the greased pig squeals away. As I sit down here in my basement, splitting my time between running the washer and dryer, and typing to you, dear reader, I wonder if this is one of those situations. Never put off tomorrow, what you could do today, especially if it could benefit a poor soul like me.

Hello, Burns, are you listening?

Therefore when the people saw the sign which Jesus had performed, they said, "This is truly the Prophet who is to come into the world." So Jesus, perceiving that they were intending to come and take Him by force to make Him king, withdrew again to the mountain by Himself alone. John 6:14f

Concluding Question:

How's the ol' Bible Holding Up?

I've always wondered (and maybe you have, too) why Bibles tend to start coming apart. Seems that you just purchase one, or one is given to you as a gift, and before you know it, the book begins to come apart. Pages start coming out in chunks, much like some folk's hair does. The spine begins to crack. Before long, the cover is free floating. What gives?

I know the answer...it's the glue.

My brother in law was, at one time, a chemist with the Borden Chemical Company. You know, the Elmer's Glue folks. What he related is that the glue used to bind the book is cheap, on the verge of junk. Why?

Quite simply, the publishers and printers know that folks, by and large, won't read it. Sure, the Bible is still one of the all-time best sellers. There are many, many publishers and printers and more versions than you can shake a stick at. Bibles are passed out at the rate of gozillions: for births, graduations from various Sunday school levels, confirmations, baptisms, VBS, weddings, Bible bowls, and the list goes on.

But no one reads it, and the printers know it. They save vast amounts of money by using the cheapest binding glue that can be found. There is nothing you, or I, can do to change this fact. There are only two items that you can do to roll the situation into your favor:

1) If your Bible falls apart, and you want to keep that particular Bible, then have it rebound.

2) If your Bible falls apart, then wear it like a badge. This is proof that you are reading it.

It's just gotta be read! Probably poor English, but you get my drift. That is the ONLY place on Planet Here that we will gather the mind of God. We can have tingly services on Sunday till the cows come home. We can give money to this work or that program till it hurts. We can volunteer for everything that comes down the pike and can dress to the nines for church, but unless we are reading our Bibles we won't know what God intends for us to know.

If reading your Bible has become a thing of the past, or was never a thing of the now, then start. I suggest starting with the Gospel of Mark and think to yourself, "Now here's a little word about God..." and watch the words come alive as you begin to read, "The beginning of the gospel of Jesus Christ, the Son of God..."

And don't forget to pray. That completes the cycle of communication: God talks, we listen (Bible reading); then we talk and God listens (prayer). Works just like two folks sitting in a coffee house.

About the Author

R F Pennington has interspersed careers, degrees and certification in oil and gas well drilling, law enforcement, clinical medicine and counseling. R F has held full time ministry positions for twelve years. He graduated from Sunset International Bible Institute and earned a Bachelors of Ministry from Theological University of America. For many years R F has focused on house church ministries and writing. R F and Dee make their empty nest in El Paso, Texas.

Published writings include this book and *Allelon: One Another, Understanding Body Life through One Another Passages* and *Jude's Letter for Today's Path, Help for the Struggling and Dealing with Ungodliness* and *The Bible Survival Manual: Mystifying to Manageable.*

All books may be obtained from online bookstores including www.bookcrafters.net.

CPSIA information can be obtained at www.ICGtesting.com
Printed in the USA
LVOW04s2116030914

402307LV00010B/94/P